T0326119

THIS BOOK IS DEDICATED TO ALL READERS WHO ARE BEING BRAVE AND LEARNING MORE ABOUT WHAT MENTAL HEALTH MEANS, NOT ONLY FOR THEMSELVES BUT FOR OTHERS AS WELL. THE MORE WE TALK, THE LESS WE WILL ALL FEEL EMBARRASSED OR ASHAMED TO SHARE OUR FEELINGS.

I HOPE *HEALTHY MIND, HAPPY YOU* CAN BE THE FIRST STEP IN HELPING OURSELVES AND EACH OTHER TO COPE WITH EVERYDAY LIFE AND BEYOND!

Published in the UK by Scholastic, 2024
1 London Bridge, London, SE1 9BG
Scholastic Ireland, 89E Lagan Road, Dublin Industrial Estate, Glasnevin, Dublin, D11 HP5F

SCHOLASTIC and associated logos are trademarks and/or registered trademarks of Scholastic Inc.

Text © Dr Emily MacDonagh, 2024
Illustrations by Josefina Preumayr and Ana Sebastián © Scholastic, 2024
Cover illustrations by Josefina Preumayr
Author photograph © Holly Clark, 2021

The right of Dr Emily MacDonagh to be identified as the author of this work has been asserted by her under the Copyright, Designs and Patents Act 1988.

Written in collaboration with Paediatric Clinical Psychologist Dr Eleanor Wells and advice from Consultant Paediatrician Dr Rebecca Mann

Dr Emily MacDonagh is represented by The CAN Group

ISBN 978 0702 32319 5

A CIP catalogue record for this book is available from the British Library.

Any website addresses listed in the book are correct at the time of going to print. However, please be aware that online content is subject to change and websites can contain or offer content that is unsuitable for children. We advise all children be supervised when using the internet.

The strategies and techniques in this book are informed by a number of different psychological therapies including Cognitive Behavioural Therapy, Acceptance and Commitment Therapy, Dialectical Behaviour Therapy and Narrative Therapy

Printed in China
Paper made from wood grown in sustainable forests and other controlled sources.

MIX
Paper from
responsible sources
FSC® C188448
FSC
www.fsc.org

3 5 7 9 10 8 6 4

www.scholastic.co.uk

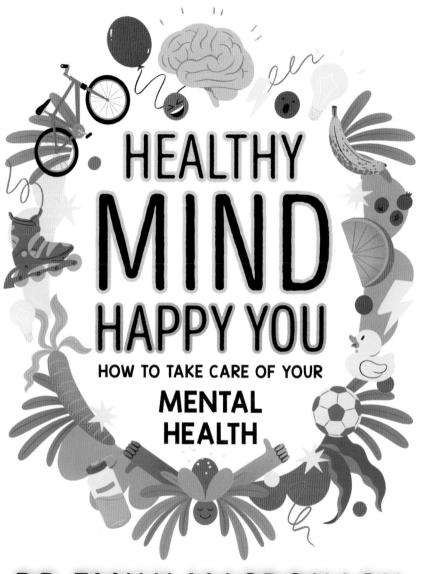

HEALTHY MIND HAPPY YOU

HOW TO TAKE CARE OF YOUR
MENTAL HEALTH

DR EMILY MACDONAGH

ILLUSTRATED BY JOSEFINA PREUMAYR
AND ANA SEBASTIÁN

■SCHOLASTIC

CONTENTS

LET'S TALK ABOUT MENTAL HEALTH

You may have heard the words mental health before, but what do they mean? Well, I like to think that mental health just means the health of your mind. Looking after your mind is just as important as keeping your body healthy.

Mental health includes your feelings, thoughts and emotions. It's about how you think and feel about yourself, about others and about the world around you. As you grow up you will notice changes in your body, but there are also changes going on in your mind. That's why looking after your mental health is so important at this time.

Knowing a bit about these changes will hopefully be really helpful. So, in this book, I'll talk all about mental health, explain what goes on in your brain and why, and help you to learn about your feelings and emotions. I'll also talk about how the changes in your body can be connected to your thoughts and feelings, and how your thoughts and feelings are connected to your behaviour and actions. All of these things can affect your mental health. I'll also show you some useful ways to cope with different feelings or situations. If there is anything you've always wanted to know about mental health, but you haven't been sure who to ask, chances are you'll find the answer here! The most important thing I hope you will take away from this book is the knowledge that everyone has their own experiences of mental health.

YOUR EXPERIENCES AND JOURNEY ARE UNIQUE – NOTHING IS RIGHT OR WRONG.

FINALLY, before you start reading, please grab a pen or pencil and some paper. When you see this icon: it means you may want to write something down. For some of these activities, it may be helpful to have a parent or adult you trust to give you a bit of a hand. They can try out the activities, too!
So, let's get started!

NICE TO MEET YOU!

I'm **DR EMILY**, and I work for the National Health Service (NHS) in the UK. I went to university for five years to study medicine, where I learned all about health, of both the body and the mind. After I finished university, I started working as a doctor, which I have done for the past eight years. For almost half of that time, I have worked with people who need help with their mental health. I wanted to write this book to share some of the things I have learnt, including some helpful hints and tips I have picked up along the way!

During my time as a doctor, I have noticed that sometimes people feel worried to ask questions about their health, especially their mental health. Sometimes they can feel silly or embarrassed. The most important thing that I want you to know is that there is no such thing as a silly question; if you are uncertain about something then the chances are that someone else is too! That is why I have included lots of questions throughout the book, so hopefully some of your own questions will be answered.

CHANGING BODIES

You may have read my books about puberty – *Growing Up for Girls* and **GROWING UP FOR BOYS**. If you haven't, no worries! Here's a quick reminder of what happens to boys and girls during puberty…

FEELING HORMONAL

First of all, why do we go through puberty in the first place? Well, the changes that happen during puberty get your body and brain ready to be an adult.

Puberty is driven by these clever things called **HORMONES**, which are like tiny chemical messengers in your body. A special part of your brain called the **PITUITARY GLAND** has a very important role to play. You can think of it like the coach of a football team, telling each part of your body what it needs to do and when. First, it tells your body to grow and change in different ways. Then it tells your emotions and thinking to mature, too, so that you're ready to deal with life as an adult.

The tricky thing is, your body often develops before your mind catches up, so you may not always feel ready for the changes! As you go through puberty, you'll discover new things about yourself and get to know your feelings. You may start becoming interested in different activities and develop close friendships with new people.

WHAT HAPPENS TO GIRLS?

Puberty usually starts a year or two earlier for girls than it does for boys. In girls' bodies it's a female hormone, called oestrogen, which has the starring role. As well as starting to grow breasts, girls will start having a period during puberty – this is when their body releases an egg every month. Hair will grow on their legs and arms, under their armpits and in the pubic area. Girls also go through growth spurts, but when you have more oestrogen in your body it begins to slow down your growth. This explains why girls stop growing sooner than boys and generally end up being shorter than men. Girls' body shapes also change: their hips get wider, and they may put on weight in areas such as the upper arms and hips. Some may also get spotty skin, and most will get more sweaty.

WHAT HAPPENS TO BOYS?

For boys, puberty is all about the hormone testosterone. They will start growing more body hair. To begin with, this can just be in their armpits and around their penis, but later they will also grow hair on their face, and may need to start shaving, as well as on their chest and tummy. Testosterone also makes them have a big growth spurt, so they get taller – and then it makes them start getting a bit musclier, too. This often doesn't happen until they are about 16–18 years old.

CHANGING EMOTIONS

As you go through puberty, the hormones in your body don't just change the way you look on the outside; they also affect the way your brain works and how you feel on the inside.

There are lots of things you will learn about your emotions when you go through puberty, such as how to understand what your feelings mean and how to tell what other people are feeling. You might also learn how to cope when you feel under pressure and how to support others when they're having a difficult time. It's completely normal to have difficulties with some of these things when you go through puberty. Lots of people are still learning about their own emotions after they become an adult, too!

BRAIN BASICS

Seeing as this book is all about mental health, it makes sense to start by talking about your **BRAIN**!

The brain is found inside the skull (the bone that you can feel when you touch the outside of your head), and it is a bit like the world's cleverest computer. It tells everything in your body what to do, even when you are asleep. It also holds all of your memories.

Most importantly, your brain is what makes you **YOU**. Just as we all look different on the outside, we each have our own special brain that is unique to us. That's why we all like different things, think different things and feel different things. Your brain makes up everything to do with you as a person: your **PERSONALITY**.

When you are very young, your brain grows really quickly. By the time you are around six years old your brain has almost reached its adult size, although it still has lots more developing to do before it works like an adult brain. A lot of this development happens during your teenage years, and carries on right through until you are in your twenties. This just goes to show how important it is to understand your own mind and take care of it as you are growing up.

BRAIN BOX

When it comes to puberty, your brain is very important. It basically organizes everything that happens to your body and prepares you to become a grown-up. Imagine your brain is kind of like your teacher, telling each member of the class (your body) what to do and when. First, it will decide when it's the best time for your body to grow and change to become more grown-up. Then it helps your thinking and emotions to get more **MATURE** too, so you can manage everything you need to live and work as an adult.

As you grow up, your brain is doing some very clever stuff. For example, it is constantly working out what information you are using and what information isn't that helpful, a bit like an electrician checking the connections between different wires. Your brain gets rid of the **"UNHELPFUL"** connections and makes the **"HELPFUL"** ones stronger. This helps your brain to be as organized as possible!

The process starts in the back part of your brain, leaving the front bit until the very last. But the frontal lobe of your brain is the part that helps you make decisions, plan things and think about what might happen if you do something (also called **CONSEQUENCES**). For example, a toddler or young child who sees a bag of sweets on the other side of the road might just run over to grab them without thinking. But, as you get older, your frontal lobe will help you remember to slow down and check for traffic first – so you might be slower getting to the sweets, but you won't get run over!

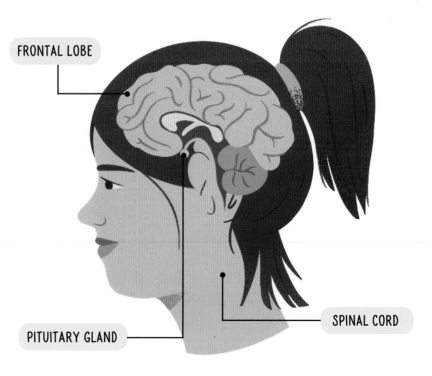

FRONTAL LOBE

SPINAL CORD

PITUITARY GLAND

At the same time, another part of your brain encourages you to start trying new things. This is really important if you are going to be a successful grown-up – you need to be prepared to learn new skills, like learning to drive, or moving to a new town to live, or getting a new job … but it also means that you might start trying new things that aren't always a good idea. It is this part of the brain that can make your teenage years a bit complicated. For instance, it's during their teenage years that some people try smoking or vaping, drinking alcohol or taking drugs for the first time. It's really important not to try new things before you understand the advantages and disadvantages, and what can happen if they go wrong.

So things can feel a bit confusing at times! You might notice that you can feel grown-up or make **"SENSIBLE"** decisions about some things, but then at other times you just can't control your actions or behaviour. This is all to do with the fact that the front part of your brain just takes a bit more time to catch up with the rest. **DON'T WORRY THOUGH, IT WILL ALL FALL INTO PLACE IN ITS OWN TIME.**

BRAIN HEALTH 101

SO WHAT THINGS KEEP OUR BRAINS HEALTHY THROUGHOUT OUR LIVES?
- Drinking lots of water to keep your body hydrated.
- Eating healthy foods that contain plenty of vitamins, minerals and nutrients.

- Getting lots of exercise and staying active.
- Protecting your brain from injury – for example wearing a helmet when you ride your scooter or bike.
- Getting enough sleep.
- Not drinking alcohol or smoking cigarettes or vaping.
- Keeping your brain active as much as possible. This could mean reading, doing art or something creative, playing an instrument, or just anything that makes you think!

The changes that happen to your brain, mind and personality during your teenage years are so important because they affect the rest of your life in a **HUGE** way. Think about how you lived your life as a child compared to how you live it now as a young person. It's pretty different, right? Well, in the future as a full blown grown-up it will all be different again!

YOUR BRAIN HAS LOTS OF GROWING UP AND CHANGING TO DO.

As children, we often think about our lives in quite a self-centred way – that means we think about ourselves first. This isn't a bad thing, as it is completely normal. As we get older, we begin to see a bigger picture of the world, and all the things that matter in it. We finish school and move on to university, college, to an apprenticeship or job. At the same time as doing all of that, we will end up thinking about moving out of our family home, to live with friends or even a partner. As we grow older, we take more and more control of our lives and become independent people with more and more confidence.

Over a few years, the **"SENSIBLE"** part of your brain (the front part) finally gains more control. As an adult you have usually tried new things, worked out which ones are OK for you, and then can get on with life, doing new things in a safe and happy way. Becoming a grown-up is a bit like going on an adventure to a really special place – there are hard parts and scary parts, but also really fun and cool parts, because you'll learn more about who you are and what you like!

The last bit to add is that all people approach these changes in different ways. Probably the biggest factor in how you do this is your personality and the ways you have seen your parents or other adults around you behaving. If you are already someone who likes doing lots of different things, and is already a bit outgoing – maybe even a risk-taker – then you are likely to feel the same in your teenage years, and could be a bit happier to experiment than some of your friends. There isn't a **"RIGHT"** way to be – it is important that you understand the advantages of trying new things as you get older, but also the risks and consequences that can happen if you get it wrong.

FIGHT, FLIGHT OR FREEZE!

To understand the way that our brains work and how this might relate to our mental health, you have to think right back … many thousands of years … to when humans lived in a very different world to the one we now know.

To survive, the earliest humans had to be able to notice **DANGER** quickly. While hunting and foraging for food, they also needed to be on the alert for predators (animals that might attack or kill them).

Those who managed to survive passed their genes from one generation to the next. As a result, humans have developed complicated systems in our brains that enable us to deal with all sorts of things. But, the part of our brains responsible for detecting threats hasn't changed for thousands of years!

That means that nowadays, our body's automatic response to threat is exactly the same as it was for our distant ancestors facing **SABRE-TOOTHED TIGERS**.

This is called the **FIGHT**, **FLIGHT** or **FREEZE** response, and it causes our bodies to get ready to fight, run away or stay incredibly still, so that we aren't detected. In many ways it is a helpful response, as it ensures that we notice threats and then get ready to respond, so we can stay alive.

Here's how it works: when your brain or body thinks that you might be in danger, hormones like **ADRENALINE** are released to get your body ready to deal with the threat. These hormones can make all sorts of changes happen in your body:

- Your heart beats faster, so that blood goes where it is needed most in your body.
- Your lungs open up to allow more air in.
- You breathe more quickly.
- More blood flows to your muscles.

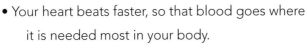

All of these things are very helpful if you need to get ready to fight an attacker or a wild animal, or run away and save yourself.

But what about when there are no sabre-toothed tigers to escape from? Life for humans now is very different to how it was all those years ago. The threat-detection part of our brain hasn't caught up with changes in the world. As a result, it can sometimes respond automatically in an unhelpful way. Yes, there are still some dangers we might come across today, but sometimes our **FIGHT, FLIGHT** or **FREEZE** response is triggered even when there isn't an actual danger before us.

We can think of our **FIGHT, FLIGHT** or **FREEZE** response as being a bit like a car alarm. It is designed to go off to let us know when there is a threat that we need to respond to, just like a car alarm sounds to let you know that someone is trying to break into a car. I bet, though, that you have heard a car alarm go off even when someone wasn't trying to break in?! Maybe somebody walked too close to the car, or the button

on the key was pressed at the wrong time, when the door was still open.

Well, the **FIGHT, FLIGHT** or **FREEZE** response can work in the same way. It can trigger us to feel worry or anxiety even when there might not be a true threat, because our body still reacts as if there really is a danger. Maybe you have to give a presentation at school, and when you find yourself in front of all those people, your body triggers the **FIGHT, FLIGHT** or **FREEZE** response. It does the things it would if you were facing something dangerous and life-threatening, even though you're not really. You might feel your heartbeat and breathing get faster, or you might get sweaty or shaky, and that can lead to you feeling very worried.

The good news is that, with practice and some handy coping strategies, you can start to explore the reasons why your internal alarm might have gone off, and work out what you need to do. We will talk a bit more about all this later on, including how the **FIGHT, FLIGHT** or **FREEZE** response can affect our mental health.

MAKING SENSE OF EMOTIONS

ASK DR EMILY

Q: What is an emotion?

A: Emotions are the different ways that we can feel. We feel different emotions in different situations, at different times of our lives and with different people. Emotions can make us feel good and at other times they can make us feel bad. All emotions are important, but they can sometimes be difficult to understand and manage. It is not always easy to know what emotion it is we are feeling, why we are feeling that way and what we can do to help cope with the feeling.

Emotions are created by the brain automatically, in response to something happening either inside of us (like thoughts or feelings in your body), or outside of us (such as different situations or interactions). When this happens, the brain sends signals around our body, which can make us feel strange or unusual sensations, cause our minds to think differently and lead us to change how we behave.

We can experience all sorts of emotions, and people can use different words to describe the same emotion. There might be times when we experience just one emotion very strongly, and others when we experience lots of feelings all at the same time. It can sometimes feel confusing, because we might notice a change in how we are feeling, but are not completely sure why, or we might not know how to explain the way we are feeling.

Spend a few moments having a think about all the different emotions you are aware of, both positive and negative. Write down all the emotions that come to mind on a piece of paper. Then, choose two different coloured pens. Using one colour, circle or colour in the emotions that you feel most often. Use the other colour to circle or colour in the emotions you would like to experience more often.

If you are finding it difficult to think of different emotions, here are some ideas:

You might notice that certain emotions seem to always come together, or shortly after one another. It is useful to notice these patterns, as it can help you to feel better prepared with ways to manage your emotions. For example, you might notice that you often feel **HAPPY** and **EXCITED** at the same time, or if you feel **RELIEVED** about something, you might then feel **CALM** afterwards. In a similar way, when we feel very **WORRIED** or **ANXIOUS** about something for a long period of time, this can also lead us to feel **LOW** or **SAD**.

Sometimes we experience emotions that don't feel **GOOD**, and that can be **CONFUSING** or **SCARY**. It might make you wonder if you are the only one feeling that way. It is important to remember that, no matter what the emotions are, other people will also have felt the same at some point.

All emotions serve a purpose, but sometimes our brains can trick us into feeling them more strongly and for longer than we need to. If you are experiencing emotions that mean you don't feel good most of the time, or if your emotions are getting in the way of you doing the things you usually enjoy, stopping you spending time with the people you care about or preventing you from doing the things you need to do (like going to school, eating, sleeping and taking care of yourself) it is important to get some extra help. Please see the **SEEKING MORE SUPPORT** section on page 125.

MIND-BODY HEALTH

Looking after your mental health is just as important as looking after your physical health. In fact, both are very closely linked! Looking after one helps to look after the other. We will learn more about this in the **SELF-CARE** section on page 77.

Feeling safe, supported and stable in our lives is also really important, as that's what gives us a strong foundation from which to cope with difficult situations and feelings. Good ways to start building this foundation include exercising, eating well, developing good sleep habits, keeping a daily routine and having people in our lives that we enjoy spending time with and trust. If we are able to maintain these things, then even when we face challenging situations in our lives or experience emotions that don't make us feel good, we will be able to cope with them much better.

UNDERSTANDING YOUR EMOTIONS

We all experience emotions differently, there is no right or wrong way to feel, and it is important to understand how you experience different emotions. Our emotions, thoughts, bodily sensations and behaviours interact together in a sort of cycle. This can be a helpful way to understand our emotional experience.

If these cycles are **POSITIVE** and allow us to do the things we want to do in our lives and be safe, supported, stable and healthy, then great!

If the cycles seem to **STOP US** from doing the things we enjoy, leave us feeling unsafe, unsupported and out of control and impact our overall physical and mental health, then it is probably sensible to try to break the cycle.

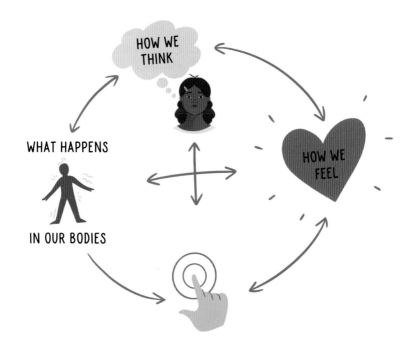

When everything is going well, this cycle of bodily sensations, thoughts, emotions and behaviours can work perfectly, helping us to live life and feel happy. But if really difficult things start happening around us, it can change the cycle. Things can get difficult to manage and it can become harder to know the best thing to do.

If you notice that you have lots of cycles that seem unhelpful, then you could speak to an adult you trust, or your doctor, to learn more about where you could find further support. You can also look at the **SEEKING MORE SUPPORT** section on page 125.

Look back at the list of emotions you made earlier. Choose **TWO** different emotions that you have experienced – include one that doesn't make you

feel good or that you can find difficult to manage. Take each emotion in turn, and use the questions below to help explore your experience of them.

My emotion or feeling is _____
I last felt this _____
I was doing _____
I was with _____
It made me feel_____
I felt it in my _____
(part of your body).
I could feel this more/less often if
I _____ (what would
you need to change to feel this way
more or less often?)

Trace the body above or sketch a body shape on to your paper and draw on the sensations you experience with each emotion. You could use a different colour for each emotion, or use a different body picture for each one – it is up to you.

Some young people notice that their body can feel **HOTTER** or **COOLER** than normal, they might notice different feelings in their tummy (like **TICKLY, EMPTY, SICK** or as if it has **BUTTERFLIES** inside of it!), perhaps they suddenly need the toilet, or their muscles feel tense in certain parts of their body. What do you notice and where?

THOUGHTS AND EMOTIONS

When we experience different emotions, our thoughts can change or how we think might be different. For example, when we feel really excited or worried, our thoughts can speed up or we might find it difficult to pick out the specific thoughts we are having. When we feel sad or worried, we can often think in a more negative or self-critical way than we do when we are feeling happy or calm.

For each emotion you chose for the previous activity, trace the outline of the brain below and write down or draw pictures to represent what you were thinking when you were last feeling that way. You can also describe ways in which your style of thinking changed with this emotion – for example, did you have lots of quick thoughts, or did it feel difficult to think? Was it difficult to notice the good things in life or things that were going well? Did your mind seem to focus on lots of negative things?

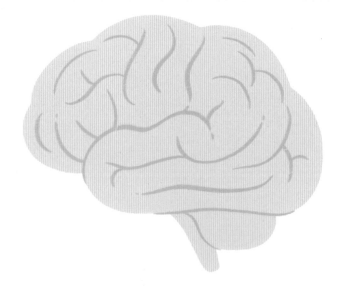

How we **THINK** and how we **FEEL** affects how we behave. In the same way, how we behave affects how we **THINK** and **FEEL**. For example, if we spend all day alone, not speaking to anyone and not really doing anything, we are likely to feel **BORED** and perhaps a bit **MISERABLE**. Whereas if we go outside, do an activity or spend time with people we trust and care about, we are more likely to feel **POSITIVE, HAPPY** or **MOTIVATED** to do more. Emotions can affect our behaviour in different ways, depending on the situation we are in. For example, we might behave differently if we feel **WORRIED** or **ANGRY** at school compared to when we are at home. It can be helpful to think about when and where we experience emotions and notice similarities and differences between them.

IF EMOTIONS WERE CHARACTERS

Emotions can feel really **BIG, OVERWHELMING** and **DIFFICULT** to manage at times. If this is the case for you, it can help to think of each emotion as its own character, which represents how you feel when you experience that emotion. This way, you can find it easier to talk about the feelings and work out ways to make the feelings bigger or smaller.

If we learn to talk about our feelings as characters separate from ourselves, it helps us to realize that the big feelings are not a problem with us, but are something that can come and go, affecting us at different times. It also becomes easier to speak about the difficult emotions and makes it easier to take control of them. Thinking about our emotions in this way can help us to understand the feelings differently and find ways to manage them. You can give your characters names and think about which ones tend to hang out together or which ones might be able to stop the more difficult feelings from hanging around too long. We can learn to talk to the characters and use our clear thinking to make it easier to cope with the difficult feelings.

Have a go at drawing your own emotional characters, and describing how they affect you; one for Anger, one for Sadness, one for Worry and one for Happiness. Here are some ideas to get that creativity flowing.

REMEMBER – as we have already explained, everyone experiences emotions differently, so your characters will be unique. There is no right or wrong way to draw your emotions.

ANGER

Anger comes unexpectedly and causes chaos! It makes me feel bad. It can make me say things I don't mean to others which causes other people to feel cross and upset. Sometimes Anger makes me want to throw things and lash out. I don't always see very clearly when it is around. Anger is loud and it can be difficult to concentrate on anything else. Often Sadness comes to visit after Anger has left.

We can learn ways to keep Anger from throwing things, whilst also letting Anger be Anger. When Anger comes, I try to take a pause and count to 10. This helps to keep Anger further away from me and gives me time to say things to Anger to quieten it and calm it down.

SADNESS

When Sadness visits,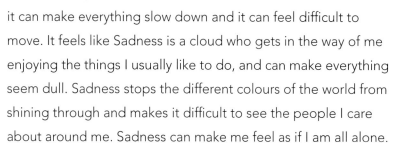
it can make everything slow down and it can feel difficult to move. It feels like Sadness is a cloud who gets in the way of me enjoying the things I usually like to do, and can make everything seem dull. Sadness stops the different colours of the world from shining through and makes it difficult to see the people I care about around me. Sadness can make me feel as if I am all alone.

We can learn ways to blow away the blue cloud of Sadness, or make it lighter so it is easier to see through and notice the world and people around us again. Sometimes other people can come to help me blow Sadness away, and often it happens more quickly when I let them help me. Once the blue cloud has lifted, I can begin to see the bright yellow of Happiness again.

WORRY

Worry can wriggle its way into my life, sometimes unexpectedly. It is a chatterbox and likes to talk very loudly, saying negative and unhelpful things. When I listen to Worry, it can grow really big and get in the way of me getting on with things in my life. Worry can block the doors and stop me from going out with my friends, going to school or parties or doing other activities that might help me to feel good or learn something new.

We can learn ways to talk back to Worry and quieten it down. We can learn ways to make Worry smaller so that we can see the world and others around us more clearly. By doing this, we can think of helpful things to say to Worry to make it wriggle away.

FOR EXAMPLE: I can learn to talk back to Worry and let it know that even though I feel a bit worried about not being with my parents while I am at school, I know I will see my friends and the teachers that help me when I am there and I will have a good time. I know I will see my parents when I come home.

HAPPINESS

Happiness makes me feel good. Every time Happiness visits, it brightens up my day and those around me. Happiness helps me to see the world and things happening around me really clearly and helps me to make plans about where I want to go next. Happiness is really powerful if it can poke through, it can push the blue cloud of Sadness and the redness of Anger away. It is pretty and fun to look at, which means that it can distract from Worry. This means Worry will eventually get bored and wriggle away. I love it when Happiness is there. I find that Happiness comes more often when I am doing regular activities which I enjoy, spending time with people I trust and looking after myself by exercising, eating good food and sleeping well.

Remember, everybody feels different emotions at different times of their lives. **ALL EMOTIONS ARE OK AND SERVE A PURPOSE**. But if you are experiencing difficult feelings a lot of the time, or they are stopping you from doing the things that you would like or need to, then it is a good idea to talk to someone and seek some extra support. Please see the **SEEKING MORE SUPPORT** section on page 125.

 So, with this in mind, I thought it would be helpful to think about a few different emotions that you might have experienced, maybe thinking about times that those emotions are positive, or a bit difficult. Then we will work through some helpful hints and tips that you can use when things are tricky. Remember your pen and paper so you can practise some of the techniques as we go along.

FEELING GOOD

What better place to start than thinking about when you feel good! Can you think of some different words to describe feeling good?

How about...

HAPPY   CALM

RELAXED   CONTENT   JOYFUL

BUZZING   EXCITED

Can you think of any more?

Now have a think about a time when you have felt any of those things. What sort of things make you feel happy, or good about yourself? Or maybe there is a person that makes you feel happy? It could be a friend, brother or sister, parent or teacher. Maybe you can think of something you have done that you really enjoyed.

For me, I love spending time outside with my family, in the garden or going for a bike ride. I also love going to the beach, feeling the sea and sand on my feet! When I was at school, I loved spending time with my friends, and played lots of hockey. I loved playing sport because I loved being part of a team with my friends. Can you think of any examples for you? You could write a list or do some drawings of these things on your paper.

How about thinking a bit more about the person, or people, who make you feel good? What is it about that person that makes you feel that way? There are many different things that you might notice about this person. They might listen to you and give you good advice. They might make sure they are there for you when you feel upset or sad. They might say nice things to you that make you feel good about yourself. You might find that you can rely on them when you need help with something, or that when you make plans together they don't let you down. They might make you laugh! Perhaps you like doing similar things and enjoy doing those things together?

SELF-CARE

So, we have thought about lots of things, people or moments when we have felt good, happy or cheerful. Just remember, no one feels like this all the time. But making time to take care of yourself is really important when it comes to feeling good. Sometimes this is called "self-care" – a fancy way of saying anything you do to take care of your body and mind.

Self-care is different for everyone. **HERE ARE SOME THINGS YOU MIGHT DO TO TAKE CARE OF YOURSELF:**

SPEND TIME WITH YOUR FRIENDS

RIDE YOUR BIKE

GO TO THE PARK

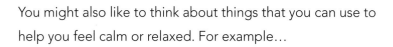

PLAY A SPORT OR DO SOME EXERCISE

DRAW A PICTURE   **READ A BOOK**

SHARE YOUR FEELINGS WITH A FRIEND

You might also like to think about things that you can use to help you feel calm or relaxed. For example…

ARE THERE ANY SMELLS THAT YOU FIND CALMING? I really like the smell of lavender (a purple flower that can be made into an oil), but you might have your own favourites. Other smells that can be quite calming are vanilla, cinnamon, mint or lemon.

CAN YOU THINK OF AN ITEM THAT HELPS YOU RELAX? Some people have a special item like a favourite toy or blanket.

WHAT ABOUT THINGS YOU CAN TOUCH THAT ARE CALMING? Things that are soft tend to be comforting, but you might think differently. Some people find that squeezing or squashing something in their hand can help distract them if they are feeling stressed or worried.

WHAT ABOUT SOMETHING YOU CAN HEAR TO HELP YOU FEEL RELAXED? The easiest example of this is listening to your favourite band or singer, but it doesn't have to be music. Some people find that listening to the sound of water running, birds singing or waves crashing on to the beach can be very soothing, too.

WHAT IS SOMETHING YOU CAN DO THAT MIGHT HELP YOU FEEL RELAXED?

Maybe kicking a ball around in the park, drawing or colouring, or swinging on the swings might calm you down, or help distract you if you're feeling anxious?

 Have a think about the things that you find calming, relaxing or soothing. Perhaps you could write down a few ideas on your piece of paper? You could keep a collection of these things in a box or drawer. You could even put some activities in there that are part of your self-care – like your favourite book or another activity that you enjoy. That way, if you want to feel calm, you can go to that place and find all the items that can help you.

If you had pulled a muscle playing with your friends at school, when you got home you might put some frozen peas on the injury and rest for the evening. Or, if you got too hot, you might have a cool shower, or put a cold towel on your head. Just as you would look after your body, you have to remember to look after your mind. The slightly tricky thing here is that sometimes it can be harder to notice what exactly you are feeling, and that therefore makes it tricky to know what to do about it.

It can be easier to say you have a headache or a sore knee than to explain to someone that you feel worried, sad or angry. That's why it's really important to get into the habit of noticing what you are feeling and noting what makes you feel good, so that when you have a day where you don't feel so great, you have an idea of what might help. This takes a bit of practice, so don't worry if you don't think you are getting it right straight away. Also, remember that no one feels good all the time. It's completely normal to have some days when you don't quite feel yourself, whether that is **SAD**, **WORRIED**, or even not quite sure what you are feeling!

MIND-BODY CONNECTION

There is a strong connection between the health of your mind and the health of your body. In other words, the way you think, feel and what you believe can have an impact on the way our body works. But it also works the other way around. The health of our physical body can also influence our mind, or mental health. You might remember we talked about this on pages 26–27 – it's called the **"MIND-BODY CONNECTION"**.

LET'S HAVE A THINK ABOUT SOME OF THE WAYS YOU CAN KEEP YOUR MIND AND BODY HEALTHY:

KEEPING ACTIVE

It's really important to try to get some physical activity into your routine. That doesn't mean you have to go to the gym or run a marathon! Just playing outside with your friends, riding your bike or doing PE are great ways to get moving. Another thing you might enjoy is playing a team sport like football, rugby or netball. Not only are team sports great to keep you active, but they can also help you meet new people or make friends. What's amazing about exercise is that it releases some helpful chemicals in your body called **ENDORPHINS**. These help you feel happy! Exercise can also improve your self-esteem – the way you feel about yourself.

HERE ARE SOME OTHER EXAMPLES OF WAYS YOU CAN KEEP ACTIVE. DO YOU HAVE ANY FAVOURITES YOU WOULD ADD TO THE LIST?

RUNNING AROUND AT LUNCHTIME **GYMNASTICS**

DANCING   **RIDING YOUR SKATEBOARD TO SCHOOL**

PLAYING HIDE AND SEEK   **PLAYING AT THE PARK**

CLIMBING A TREE

BODY FUEL

All this talk of exercise is making me feel hungry! Did you know that the food you eat is also very important for your mental health? While it's OK to have a special treat every now and then, it's a good idea to try to eat a balanced diet. This basically means have a little bit of everything and not too much of one thing. Trying to eat some fruit and vegetables and avoiding foods very high in sugar is a good place to start.

It's also important to drink plenty of water. Believe it or not, a lot of your body is made up of water **(ROUGHLY TWO THIRDS!)**, so it is very important to make sure there is enough of it. Drinking water helps nearly every system in your body: it helps to digest your food, helps your kidneys to work well and even helps your brain to be on top form! Try to drink between six and eight cups of water each day (around one and a half litres) if you can, and more if you are doing sports or exercise, as you will lose some of your body's water through sweating.

If you think about it, it makes perfect sense that it is important to eat and drink well. Your body and mind is fuelled by everything you eat and drink, so put some good stuff in there to help yourself feel as strong and healthy as possible!

BODY IMAGE

Having a healthy body image means feeling happy and confident about your body and accepting the way that you look. Feeling good about your body can help you feel happier overall. A good way to help your self-esteem is to focus on yourself as a whole person, and try not to focus on the things about your body that you might not like as much.

You also need to remember that you are not just the way your body looks – your personality and the things you are good at are a massive part of who you are.

Remember that others will see you as a whole package, not just what's on the outside.

There are things you can do to keep your body image healthy, like keeping active and trying to eat a balanced diet as we have just mentioned. This doesn't mean you can't eat things that you like, just consider swapping some things for healthier options.

SLEEP

As well as fuelling your body with the right foods and drinking enough water, it's also very important to get enough sleep. This is especially important during puberty and in your teenage years. This is because your body and mind are growing, changing and developing at a rapid rate!

Here's an amazing fact – did you know that a teenager's body clock actually shifts forwards by one or two hours compared to children or adults? This means that teenagers naturally stay awake longer and wake up later. As part of puberty, your brain also starts producing more growth hormones – mainly at night, when you are asleep. This is part of the reason why teenagers and young people need more sleep than adults.

TEENAGERS AND YOUNG PEOPLE NEED SLEEP TO:
- Produce more growth hormone to help grow and stay physically fit and strong.
- Keep up energy levels.
- Concentrate and learn at school.

- Be able to remember things.
- Interact with others in a positive way.
- Feel more able to manage any stress or worries.

If you're not getting enough sleep it can make it more difficult to concentrate at school, get on with friends, or feel motivated to do things you need to do. It can also make you feel more emotional, or perhaps you might notice you feel grumpy or a bit "moody". Being very tired all the time can also make it hard to behave as you'd like, pay attention and get along with others. Feeling tired all the time or having difficulties with your sleep could be a sign that your mental health might need some attention.

There are lots of things that can make it difficult to sleep when you are growing up. Being busy at school, taking exams, or a hectic after-school schedule might cut into your sleep time. Also, believe it or not, the light that comes from phones, tablets or televisions actually tricks your brain into thinking it is still daytime! This can stop your body producing chemicals like melatonin, which controls your body's sleep/wake cycle. Melatonin is produced at night (when it gets dark) and is part of what makes you feel sleepy. So if you're using your phone late at night, or watching some late-night TV, your melatonin levels might be lower and you might struggle to get to sleep. Remember what I said about teenagers naturally going to sleep later and waking up later? This is fine, until you have to get up early for school! Going to sleep later but then having to wake up early can mean that teenagers don't get the sleep that their body needs.

TOP TIPS FOR A GOOD NIGHT'S SLEEP!
HERE A FEW THINGS YOU CAN TRY TO MAKE SURE YOU ARE GETTING A REALLY GOOD NIGHT'S SLEEP:

- Avoid sugary or caffeinated drinks after lunch (these aren't actually good for your physical health at any time of day!)
- Try not to go on your phone or tablet for at least one hour before bedtime.
- Try not to do exciting activities later in the evening. Instead of computer games or loud music, try calming music, guided meditations, audio books or sleep sounds.
- Have a regular evening routine, this could include running a warm bath, reading a book and having a warm drink of milk.
- Try to have your room as dark as possible at night. This will help your body to recognize that it is time for sleep so it will release the sleep chemicals.
- Try not to go to bed hungry, and don't eat just before you go to bed either.

So, we have thought about feeling good, what that means to you and what things might help you feel good. Next let's think about some other emotions…

FEELING WORRIED

Everyone feels worried sometimes, even grown-ups! It's possible to feel worried about things that have already happened, things that are about to happen, or things that might happen further in the future. Feeling worried is an extremely common emotion and one that we will all experience at various stages throughout our lives. In fact, feeling worried is completely normal in some situations! There aren't many people who wouldn't feel worried at all about moving house, or starting a new school or job, for example.

You may have heard people use other words to describe feeling worried, like:

ANXIETY   FEAR

SCARED   FEELING ANXIOUS   PANICKED

NERVOUSNESS   STRESSED

Everyone will have a slightly different way of describing how they feel when they are worried, whether that is one of the words listed here, or something different. Some people might say they have **"BUTTERFLIES"** in their tummy. As we have said before, it is important to try to work out how it feels for you.

WHAT IS ANXIETY?

Anxiety is our body's way of alerting us to danger and keeping us safe when we are under threat (remember the **FIGHT**, **FLIGHT** and **FREEZE** response we talked about earlier?). When we are anxious, we often notice physical symptoms, like our heart beating faster, muscle tension, **"BUTTERFLIES"** or a churning feeling in our stomach.

Here are some examples of how anxiety might feel in your body.

REMEMBER, EVERYONE IS DIFFERENT AND MIGHT EXPERIENCE THESE FEELINGS IN A DIFFERENT WAY, OR IN A DIFFERENT PART OF THEIR BODY.

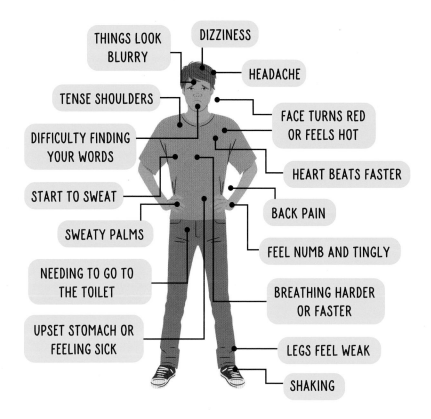

THINGS LOOK BLURRY

DIZZINESS

HEADACHE

TENSE SHOULDERS

FACE TURNS RED OR FEELS HOT

DIFFICULTY FINDING YOUR WORDS

HEART BEATS FASTER

START TO SWEAT

BACK PAIN

SWEATY PALMS

FEEL NUMB AND TINGLY

NEEDING TO GO TO THE TOILET

BREATHING HARDER OR FASTER

UPSET STOMACH OR FEELING SICK

LEGS FEEL WEAK

SHAKING

Too much or too little stress and anxiety can be unhelpful. Sometimes we need to feel some stress to help us prepare and concentrate, and to succeed in tasks like exams or sports.

Our brain is very good at linking two things together. For the most part, this can be helpful, but sometimes it can become unhelpful. If we feel anxiety in a certain situation, our brain can make a link with that situation and that worried feeling. This means that similar situations in the future can lead us to feel worried even if the situation is not the same…

Imagine you went into your garden shed yesterday to get your bike and unexpectedly saw a mouse! It took you by surprise and made you jump! Today, you need to go back into the shed, but you notice you feel worried. You feel worried in case another mouse takes you by surprise – your brain has made a link between the shed and feeling worried. This is an unhelpful link because it isn't actually the shed that caused the worry, it was the surprise visit from the mouse!

ASK DR EMILY

Q: Can you worry too much?

A: The first thing to say in answer to this question is that what one person feels is too much worrying compared to another might be very different. But, worrying too much can become a problem if it is stopping you from being able to enjoy yourself or preventing you from doing things that you would like or need to do. For example, some people find that their feelings of worry are very strong, so they feel nervous or anxious a lot of time. Sometimes, people begin to stop doing (or avoid doing) things that they think might make them anxious. This might mean that they stop doing things that they enjoy, like playing sport or spending time with friends. Another thing that can happen is where something makes you feel much more anxious than it really should – similar to what we have talked about with the **FIGHT**, **FLIGHT** and **FREEZE** response. For example, it is normal to feel worried if you are speaking in front of your class at school, but if you feel sick, sweaty, notice your heart racing, can't sleep the night before, or even avoid doing it entirely, then that might be quite difficult for you. Or perhaps everyday activities are making you feel more scared or worried than your friends – for example, feeling very worried about crossing the road or riding your bike, so you avoid doing these things completely. This is particularly important if these activities are something you enjoy doing and you feel unable to do them.

If you think this sounds familiar, then it is a good idea to speak to someone about it so they can help you think about what can be done to help. That could be a parent, teacher or another adult you trust.

HOW DOES WORRY FEEL?

When you get worried or anxious, your body releases the stress hormone **ADRENALINE** which we heard about earlier. This has the effect of increasing your heart rate, it makes you breathe faster, it can make you feel like you have butterflies in your tummy, go red, feel shaky or even develop a rash. Many people notice these symptoms when they are anxious or stressed. You are simply noticing the effects of adrenaline on your body.

Adrenaline can make you feel pretty terrible, but it doesn't last long in the body. If you are able to understand what is going on and stay calm, those physical feelings of worry will settle quite quickly.

Take a moment to think about a point in your life when you felt worried, anxious or stressed. **WHAT WAS HAPPENING AT THE TIME?** Perhaps you had fallen out with a friend, moved house or school, or maybe you were finding schoolwork a bit tricky? Now try to remember what you felt at that time. **DID YOU FEEL ANYTHING IN YOUR BODY, FOR EXAMPLE ANY OF THE THINGS SHOWN IN THE DIAGRAM ON PAGE 49?** You could even draw your own body and note down whereabouts in your body you noticed anything.

WORRISOME THOUGHTS

When we feel worried, the way we think can change. We can start to have lots and lots of thoughts zooming around our mind that can feel difficult to keep track of, or we might find it difficult to concentrate on other things, because all we can think about is one **GIANT** worry – every time we try to think about something else, the big worry barges in!

Different parts of our brain communicate to help make sense of our emotions clearly. These parts of our brain help us to decide if the emotions we experience are because of a real threat in our environment or not. When we experience strong emotions, it can make this communication in the brain more difficult, and we are unable to make sense of what we are feeling or think clearly about things. When we feel worried, the thinking part of our brains can focus on it too much and can make the worry even bigger than it would have been on its own.

There are some really common ways of thinking that we can all find ourselves falling into when we feel worried. I have mentioned a few of these below. It can be really useful to try to notice these unhelpful thinking patterns. If we notice when we are thinking in that way, it is easier to stop, try to change it and take more control over the way we feel.

THINKING THAT THE WORST THING WILL DEFINITELY HAPPEN

This is also known as **CATASTROPHIZING**. When we feel worried about something it is easy to jump to the worst possible conclusion. **FOR EXAMPLE**, if we feel worried about a test at school, our mind might begin to think: "If I fail this test, I will fail school and I won't ever get a job." Worries have an unhelpful way of getting bigger and bigger very quickly. If we don't keep them in check, they can let us believe that terrible things will happen if we do those things we feel worried about. But really, we all get things wrong sometimes! In fact, this is a really important part of us learning and developing. Getting a question wrong doesn't mean that we will fail all of our school exams, and failing a maths or English test certainly doesn't mean we won't ever get a job! The worried feeling, however, can make us believe that those things are true.

BECOMING A MIND READER

When we feel worried, we often believe that we know what others are thinking. Our beliefs about what other people are thinking can then affect how we feel in different situations or how we think about ourselves. But in real life, no one can read other people's minds. When we feel worried about something, we are more likely to guess that someone is thinking negatively or in a way that supports our worry. By doing this, it sets us up to experience things (such as situations, events or interactions) in a more negative way and a way that can keep our worry going. For example, **"IF I GET THE ANSWER WRONG, PEOPLE WILL THINK I AM SILLY AND WON'T WANT TO BE MY FRIEND ANY MORE."** Or, **"SHE DIDN'T REPLY TO MY MESSAGE BECAUSE SHE THINKS I AM BORING."** Sometimes people call this **"OVERTHINKING"** – meaning we take something small, and think it through again and again until it becomes a much bigger issue than it ever was to begin with – we overthink it into something **BIG**.

SEEING INTO THE FUTURE

When we are worried, our minds can start trying to guess what will happen later or in the future. For example, we might think things like: "THERE IS NO POINT IN ME TRYING TO DO THIS, BECAUSE I WON'T BE ABLE TO," or "I'M NOT GOING TO GO TO THE PARTY BECAUSE NO ONE WILL TALK TO ME." But we are not able to predict the future in this way, so it is an unhelpful way of thinking, which stops us doing things that will almost certainly be fine.

AVOIDING THINGS WE NEED OR WANT TO DO BECAUSE OF WORRIES

Worries can feel really unpleasant and none of us like to feel worried. One of the most common ways to respond to worries is to avoid the thing, situation or person we are feeling worried about.

This helps us to stop the worried feeling and may make us feel better for a short period of time. **BUT**, avoiding the situation or thing that was making us feel worried never lets us challenge the worries we have. This is really important because if we always avoid things, we will feel even more worried every time we are faced with it. If I worry that if I go to a party, no one will speak to me and I will have a terrible time, I might decide not to go to the party. So then, I never get to find out if my belief about what will happen actually happens, or whether my worry is, in fact, just a worry and not a truth! Without going to the party, even if the worry on that occasion goes away, I will never get the chance to learn that parties are fun and I enjoy them when I go.

HOW TO MANAGE WORRY

One of the most important things to remember about our emotions is that they don't stay the same for ever. They are always changing. This means that even when we feel worried and think that the feeling is just going to get worse and worse over time, this is just our worried mind making us think that way. What actually happens is that the worried feeling might get bigger to start with, but eventually it will stop getting worse and then start to get smaller. If we just left the worry for enough time, it would shrink down on its own.

But sometimes worry can make things really difficult, especially if you are worrying a lot of the time. So let's look at some strategies and suggestions that might help you cope when you feel worried.

There are lots of different ways to manage worry and different things will work for different people. The most important thing is to try out the different strategies below and work out what suits you. Sometimes it is helpful to try a strategy a couple of times before you decide if you find it helpful or not. These suggestions can be used in specific situations or in daily life when general worries may come and go.

WORKING OUT YOUR WORRIES

The first step to managing your worries is understanding them. Hopefully, reading this book is helping you to make sense of how worries can affect the way we feel, think and behave. It is important to work out some of the main things that are contributing to your worries so that it can be easier to choose strategies to help manage them. It might not be possible to identify everything you are feeling worried about, but I am sure you can definitely think of some of the most common worries you have!

 **GIVE THESE IDEAS A GO TO HELP YOU WORK OUT AND COPE WITH YOUR WORRIES.**

THE WORRY PIZZA

Draw a picture of a pizza, cut into slices. On each slice write or draw a picture of something that you often feel worried about or that has recently worried you. You can add different toppings to the slices. You could even make the slices different sizes, depending on how big a worry that particular thing is to you.

A SPECIAL WORRY BOX

 If you find talking about your worries a bit difficult, try writing about or drawing them instead. You could decorate a special box, where you can put these worries once you have written or drawn them. This box is somewhere you can keep the worries safe, without having to hold them in your mind all the time. When you feel ready or able to, you can take them out of the box and think about ways to manage the worries. You might find that after putting them in the box for a little while, the worries have actually become smaller!

Another helpful thing to do is to let someone you trust know about the box. If you are happy for them to, they can then have a look at what you have put in the box, so that they learn about your worries without you having to explain them. They can then help you think about different ways of managing the worries. You can always agree a time each week to go through the box together. This will give you the chance to start feeling more confident in talking about your worries with someone else, and help you think together about different ideas to tackle them.

CONTROLLED BREATHING

One of the most helpful ways to manage the feelings we get in our body when we experience worry is to **BREATHE!** Breathing helps us to feel calm and relaxed. It is a great strategy as it can be practised anywhere and at any time. Here are two ideas to help you practise controlled breathing and learn to calm and slow your breath, that scientists have proven help with managing worry.

SQUARE BREATHING

Imagine a square box, or find something that is shaped like a square in the room you are in (maybe a window, a computer screen or a page in your book). Follow the edge of the square with your eyes (or in your mind if you are imagining it) as you breathe in for four counts, hold your breath for four counts, and breathe out for four counts – then start again.

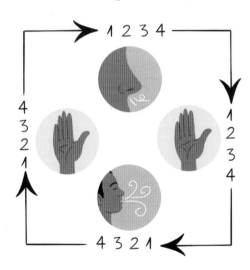

Once you have practised calm and slow breathing, the next step is to try making the out-breath longer than your in-breath. Start off by trying to breathe in for four counts and out for five or six counts.

FIVE-FINGER BREATHING

1 Hold up one hand with the fingers outstretched.
2 With your other hand, make a point with your index finger (first finger next to the thumb).

3 Starting at the bottom of the thumb, use your index finger to trace up the outside of your thumb to the very tip, while slowly breathing in through your nose.

4 When you get to the tip, trace down the other side of your thumb to the base of it, while breathing out through your mouth.

5 Repeat for all fingers until you have traced around your whole hand.

CREATE A SAFE SPACE

What is around us can affect how we feel emotionally. If you can, try to create a special space in your home where you can feel calm and relaxed. You might make this a really comfortable place with cushions and soft blankets or decorate it with your favourite colours, photographs or drawings. You can keep special objects or your **SELF-SOOTHE BOX** (see below) here, so you can easily access it when you feel worried.

If you feel worried when you are away from home, you could always try closing your eyes and thinking about your safe space, imagining you are there. Doing this can help you to feel calmer.

SELF-SOOTHE BOX

Take a look back at the **FEELING GOOD** section beginning on page 36. What were the different things you noticed that helped you to feel good, calm and relaxed? These might be activities or things to do, sensory objects that you like to touch or smell, or photographs or special objects that remind you of important and positive people, places or experiences you have had. Put together a box or bag of these things. This can become your special toolbox, which you can go to when you are feeling worried. Make sure you keep it in a safe space, which you can access easily, because when you feel really worried it can be difficult to think clearly and so it needs to be obvious to you at that time.

HERE ARE SOME EXAMPLES OF THINGS PEOPLE MIGHT INCLUDE IN THEIR SELF-SOOTHE BOXES:

- Colouring or drawing materials
- Stress balls
- Ribbons
- Soft toys
- Scented sprays or perfumes
- Favourite music
- Photographs of important and positive people or places.

THE WORRY TREE

Sometimes there are practical things that you can do to help make a worry smaller. The Worry Tree can help us to think about which worries we might be able to solve and which we need to manage in a different way. When you notice you feel worried, follow the questions on the Worry Tree to guide you to how to respond.

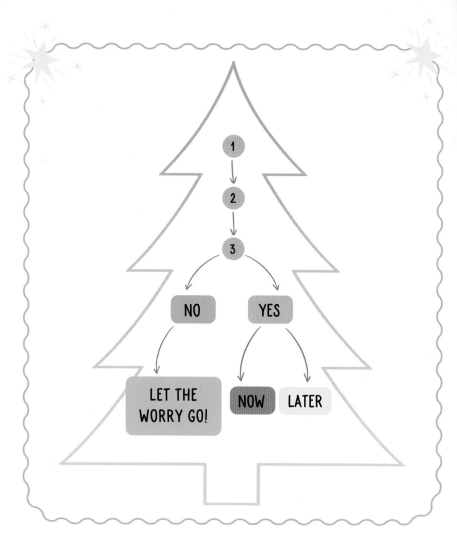

1. Notice your worry

2. Ask yourself what it is you are feeling worried about. (You could always use your worry pizza to help you work this out if you are unsure!)

3. Ask yourself if this is a problem at the moment? Can you do anything about the thing you are worried about? Or is it something out of your control or something that hasn't happened yet? (WE CALL THIS HYPOTHETICAL.)

NO

- Let the worry go – it is out of your control!
- Find something to do to help you change your focus of attention/distract yourself (see **DISTRACTION** on page 64).

YES (current problem)

- It's time to create an action plan! **WHAT**: think of some ideas that you can use to try to solve the problem. **WHEN**: when can you try out these ideas? Is it straight away or do you need to plan a time for this later on? **HOW**: what or who might you need to help you try out these ideas?

NOW

- Carry out the action plan!
- Let the worry go – you have tried all you can do at this point!
- Find something to do to help you change your focus of attention/distract yourself (see **DISTRACTION** on page 64).

LATER

- Plan when you are going to try out your problem-solving ideas.
- Let the worry go – you can't do any more until it is time to try out your ideas.
- Find something to do to help you change your focus of attention/distract yourself (see **DISTRACTION** on page 64).

RELAXATION

If you look back at the cycles we talked about earlier on pages 27–28, you will remember that our body experiences physical sensations when we feel different emotions. Often, when we are worried, our body can feel tight, tense and even restless. Relaxation can help our bodies to release tension and help us to feel calmer. If our bodies feel calmer, our minds will start to feel calmer too! There are lots of different ways we can relax. **HERE ARE SOME IDEAS:**

- Have a warm bath or shower.
- Go for a walk, swim or bike ride.
- Read a book or watch a film you enjoy.
- Try drawing, colouring or painting.

DISTRACTION

If our worries feel really big, it is not always easy to relax. You might find that using some **DISTRACTION TECHNIQUES** first will help make the worry smaller, to then allow you to try some relaxation strategies.

HERE ARE SOME IDEAS:

- Counting backwards from 100. You could then make it more challenging by counting backwards in 5s or even 3s!
- List an animal starting with each letter of the alphabet, for example, aardvark, bull, cow. You could then try this with other categories too, like favourite foods, sports or countries.
- Watch a funny YouTube clip.
- Listen to your favourite song.

MINDFULNESS

Mindfulness is a skill that many people practise as a way of helping them to manage with worry, for coping when things are uncertain or they are worried about the future. Mindfulness helps us try to focus on what is happening now, and not get caught up in what happened in the past or what might happen in the future.

It is really common to notice the worrying thoughts creeping in whilst you are trying to focus on something else. If this happens, just notice the worry and try to bring your focus back to the exercise. There are lots of different mindfulness exercises you can try. Take a look at the ideas below – remember, it is important to **PRACTISE MINDFULNESS** – it is not always easy!

GROUNDING – 5, 4, 3, 2, 1

This technique can be really useful when we feel overwhelmed by our emotions. It encourages us to use our senses to help us focus on what is happening right now in the moment and not get distracted by the past or the future. It lets focus on our surroundings and feel better connected with where we are and ourselves.

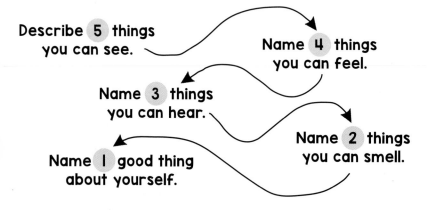

Describe **5** things you can see.

Name **4** things you can feel.

Name **3** things you can hear.

Name **2** things you can smell.

Name **1** good thing about yourself.

MINDFUL ACTIVITY

Almost anything that you need to do during your day can be used to practise mindfulness. For example if you have a shower, try spending a few moments focusing on the following:

- What does the water feel like falling on your skin or your head? Is it warm or cool? Does it feel the same on different parts of your body?
- What does your shower gel or shampoo smell like?
- What can you hear during the shower? Can you hear the water falling on the shower floor or other sounds in the bathroom?
- What can you see? Can you see steam forming on the mirror or window? Or different shadows on the shower curtain?

Worries come and go. Some hang around for longer and some are bigger and more overwhelming than others. You will find some of the strategies described here work better for you and some you might not like as much. **THAT IS ABSOLUTELY OK!** You may also find that some strategies work well with some worries, but not others. Often this depends on how strong your worries are – some strategies work best for smaller worries and others for when worries feel really big. For example, if we are feeling really overwhelmed with worries, we might find that practising some controlled breathing or relaxation is needed before you can start thinking about the details of your worries and different ideas to solve them.

Try using the thermometer below to think about the things that you worry about most often and how much they bother you. Next to each level of worry, write a strategy you think may be helpful to manage it.

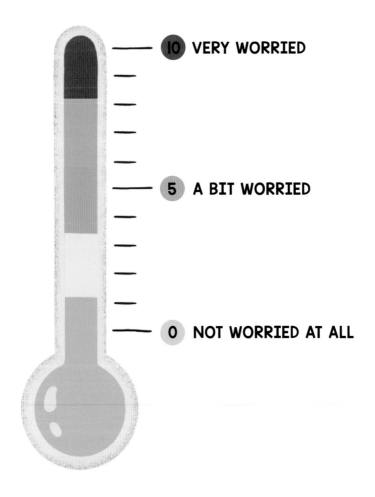

10 **VERY WORRIED**

5 **A BIT WORRIED**

0 **NOT WORRIED AT ALL**

FEELING SAD

We have already thought about feeling good and feeling worried. But what about another emotion – sadness? A bit like the other emotions we have already thought about, everyone in the world will experience feeling sad at one time or another. It is a normal emotion shared by all human beings.

Let's have a think about other ways to describe feeling sad:

UPSET

UNHAPPY

MISERABLE

FEELING DOWN

FEELING LOW

FEELING FLAT

DEPRESSED

SORROW

Feeling sad often comes from the loss of something or someone important to you. In other words, when you lose something that you care about. An example might be falling out with a friend **("LOSING" A FRIENDSHIP)** or moving house **("LOSING" YOUR OLD HOME, FRIENDS OR SCHOOL)**. Other things that might make you feel sad could include being bullied **(OR SEEING SOMEONE ELSE BEING BULLIED)**, or other difficulties at home or at school. Obviously there are lots of different things that can make us feel sad. Often, feeling worried and feeling sad can go together, for example if you feel very worried about your friends or schoolwork, in time that could also make you feel sad.

Sometimes, when we feel sad, it can also make our bodies feel different. Everyone will describe this in their own way, but some examples include:

- Feeling heavy – in your head, stomach or chest.
- Headaches or tummy pains – or pain in other areas of your body.
- Feeling tired or not having much energy.
- Feeling "numb" – this is when we don't really feel anything. Our bodies can feel heavy or empty or when we don't experience any changes in how our body feels, even when lots of things are changing or happening around us.
- Crying or feeling tearful.

HOW DOES SADNESS FEEL?

Can you think of a time that you felt sad? What was happening to you when you felt like that? Where did you feel it in your body (trace and label the below diagram)? Did you feel any other emotions at the same time?

Most people would say that they don't like to feel sad, and would probably prefer to feel other emotions, like happiness or excitement. But you might be interested to know that even emotions that we think are negative, like sadness, are normal and even important. Scientists actually think that we experience sadness for a reason. In fact, in some circumstances, it is thought to be helpful. For example, when we feel sad, this encourages us to speak to other people, comfort each other, and by doing this we build connections and relationships with others around us. Think of how you would react if you saw a friend at school sitting alone and crying – you would notice they are upset by observing their behaviour and body language, and that might encourage you to go and talk through what is upsetting them. You might ask if there is anything you can do to help or comfort them. Many years ago **(WAY BACK IN HISTORY)**, it would have been very important to have strong connections with other humans in your tribe, to protect and look after each other.

Another helpful thing about **SADNESS** is that you could even think about it as a little alert for your body. Feeling sad might tell your body that you are in a difficult or unfamiliar situation. This can make you take a step back and think about what might have made you feel that way. Stepping back and considering what has happened to make you feel sad can be helpful for the future, as you will learn over time which behaviours and situations might end up making you feel sad, and learn how to manage them. This is all part of learning how to handle difficult situations, or losses that you might come across in your life. So, sadness can help you learn to **ADAPT** and **LEARN** how to deal with loss. Sometimes we call this **BUILDING RESILIENCE**, which literally means learning to deal with difficult situations in a healthy way and move forwards.

HOW CAN I BUILD RESILIENCE?

We all develop our own ways to build resilience throughout our lives. Even grown-ups are still learning how to do this!

HERE ARE SOME OF MY TOP TIPS FOR BUILDING RESILIENCE:

- Be positive about yourself, even when you make mistakes. We all make mistakes, it is just important to think about what you learn from them and how you would do it differently next time.
- Keep trying! Even when something is really tricky, don't give up. Remember, you can only do your best, and your best **IS** good enough.
- Try to think positive thoughts.
- Take care of yourself (see page 38 about **SELF-CARE**).
- Try to accept that things change throughout life – although it's hard sometimes, you will get used to change and see the positives that can come of it.
- Ask for help if you need it – although it's always good to give things a try by yourself, it's so important that you speak to someone when you need support or advice.
- Keep positive and supportive people around you – like kind and supportive friends who you know you can rely on.
- Help others when they need you. Helping other people to build their own resilience is so important and it also helps you to feel good about yourself.

If you are faced with a difficult situation, perhaps ask yourself some of these questions:

"WHAT COULD I DO DIFFERENTLY HERE THAT MIGHT MAKE THINGS EASIER OR BETTER?"

"WHO MIGHT I BE ABLE TO ASK FOR ADVICE OR HELP?"

"I DON'T THINK I CAN CHANGE ANYTHING ABOUT THIS SITUATION, BUT CAN I THINK CAREFULLY ABOUT SOMETHING I CAN CHANGE?"

"CAN I BREAK DOWN THIS PROBLEM INTO A FEW PIECES THAT FEEL EASIER TO MANAGE?"

"HAVE I BEEN IN THIS SITUATION BEFORE, OR SOMETHING SIMILAR? WHAT WAS HELPFUL OR NOT SO HELPFUL THEN?"

ASK DR EMILY

Q: What's the difference between sadness and anger?

A: Sometimes we can cover up sadness with other emotions, like anger. Let's think of an example – you overhear someone at school saying something unkind about you. You might think – "I feel so angry with that person for saying that!" But actually, let's think about the feelings you might have in this situation. Underneath the anger, you may feel sad or upset that someone had spoken about you in that way. You might feel that you have done something wrong, or wonder why that person doesn't like you. Think back to what we said

73

about seeing someone sad or upset, and how you would probably be drawn towards them to comfort them. But if someone looked angry, you would probably avoid going too near them! This just goes to show one of the differences between anger and sadness, and why it is important to try to notice those differences in yourself. We will learn more about anger and how you can manage it later on.

ASK DR EMILY

Q: Am I feeling too sad?

A: We have talked about how sadness is a normal human emotion and how it can actually be helpful. But if we feel very sad, or feel sad for long periods of time, then it probably isn't helpful any more.

A good way to think of this is that if you are feeling very sad a lot of the time, and especially if it is stopping you enjoying things or having an impact on your life in other ways, then it may be time to get some help or support. Sometimes, when we feel very sad for a long time, we can experience other things, such as having difficulty concentrating, remembering things, sleeping or feeling tired a lot, changes in appetite or not feeling motivated to do things. Other things that someone might experience are low self-esteem (not feeling good about themselves) or feeling guilty about things.

Sometimes people take themselves away from their friends or family or stop doing things they would usually enjoy. Also, as we talked about earlier, feeling sad can go along with feeling worried or anxious. If any of this sounds familiar, then it is really important to speak to a grown-up you trust, like a parent or teacher, to get some advice and support.

SAD THOUGHTS

When we feel sad, the way we think can change. We can find ourselves focusing on only negative things and ignoring anything more positive that might be happening around us. We might find it difficult to concentrate on anything other than feeling sad or what is making us feeling sad. We know that when we feel very strong emotions, communication in the brain can be more difficult and we are less able to think clearly.

Just as when we feel worried, there are some common ways of thinking that we can fall into when we feel sad. I've mentioned some of these below. It can be useful to try to notice these unhelpful thinking patterns when they happen. If we notice when we are thinking that way, it's good to try to change it and take control over how we feel, so that things can get better.

GLOOMY GOGGLES

When we feel sad, we can find it difficult to notice the positive things that are happening around us, or nice things that are being said to us. Our brains seem to focus only on the things that aren't going so well or interpret things being said to us in a critical or negative way. When we notice that we might be wearing our "GLOOMY GOGGLES", it can be helpful to pause and think about what is actually happening or being said, and decide if it really is all negative, or whether our goggles might be clouding the more positive things.

BEING UNKIND TO YOURSELF

Sometimes when we feel sad, we can be really hard on ourselves. We can think that the things we do or say are wrong, think that we haven't done something well enough or think we aren't good enough. A lot of the time, these thoughts aren't true and don't actually describe what really happened or how other people would have described things. When we feel sad for a long time, it can be difficult to notice the things we have done well or the positives in life (because of our gloomy goggles!), and this can lead us to start thinking negatively about ourselves.

PUTTING PRESSURE ON OURSELVES

When we feel sad, our thoughts can not only become critical (for example, thinking we are bad or wrong), but we can also start putting pressure on ourselves. We might put pressure on ourselves to do more or to always be perfect in everything. We might start thinking unhelpful things like: "I SHOULD HAVE..." or "I MUST..." The problem with thinking in this way is that it can lead us to get the wrong idea about what is likely to happen, and when those things often don't happen, it can leave us feeling more disappointed and sad. The pressure these thoughts put on us can keep sadness going and also make worry get stronger too.

HOW TO MANAGE SADNESS

Just as we spoke about tricks and habits you can learn to help you manage things when you feel worried, there are some simple things you can put in place to help when you are feeling sad. Keep on reading for some specific examples…

SELF-CARE AND THINGS THAT HELP YOU FEEL GOOD

One of the most important things to do when you are feeling sad is to keep trying to do the things that usually help you to feel good. Have a think back to the **FEELING GOOD** section on page 36. What sort of things did you think of that made you feel good? When we feel sad, we can often feel less motivated to go out and do the things we normally enjoy or spend time with the people we usually like to see. Even though we might not feel like it, it's really important to try to make plans to do these things. Often, if we can push ourselves to go out and do an activity, or speak to a friend, it can help make the sad feeling a bit smaller and even start to help us feel good again.

It can be helpful to make a list of some of the activities you usually enjoy and keep this in your **SELF-SOOTHE BOX** (see **MANAGING WORRY** on page 56). Then you can look at it when you feel sad and choose one or two things that you can try to do.

The **SELF-SOOTHE BOX** should also contain lots of things that help you to feel calm, relaxed and perhaps remind you of positive or happy memories. Although we talked about it in the **MANAGING WORRY** section, your **SELF-SOOTHE BOX** is actually a really good tool to use for any of your difficult emotions. Try to have lots of different things in your box that might suit your different emotions. Keep it somewhere safe and easy to access, so you can get to it when you are feeling sad.

ROUTINE AND PLANNED ACTIVITIES

Keeping a good routine every day can be really helpful for experiencing positive moods and feeling good as much as possible. However, when we feel sad, we often don't feel like doing very much (our motivation goes down or it can seem to disappear completely!). Creating an activity timetable for what you will do each day can be a really helpful way to slowly start to build your motivation back up again. Start off by trying to plan one activity a day, then increasing to more activities each day when you can. You should focus on doing activities that you usually enjoy or that can bring you a sense of achievement (like a hobby, seeing friends or learning something new), as well as things that you need to do (like **TIDYING YOUR ROOM** or your **HOMEWORK**).

Lots of people put off doing things because they don't feel motivated. Often, they can think that they will do it at a time when they do feel more motivated. Unfortunately, motivation doesn't just build up on its own … we need to start doing something in order to build the motivation ourselves. Think of it like making a snowman … you might wake up one morning and there is lots of snow all around you. The snow doesn't automatically form itself into a snowball and then another, becoming a snowman on its own. You have to go outside, start collecting the snow, roll it over and over and over, until it is big enough for the base. Then you start again to make two more balls for the head and body. Only then does it begin to look a bit like a snowman. It's the same for motivation – you need to do a bit to build up your motivation to do more things.

GET MOVING!

Remember what I said about the benefits of exercise and getting your body moving on pages 41–42? Moving our bodies, getting fresh air and doing physical activity is proven to help us feel good. When you feel sad, your motivation is likely to be low (or non-existent!). Start off with smaller or easier goals. Try going for a walk or kicking a football about outside for ten minutes to begin with, and then slowly increase what you do. Trying to do physical activity with other people can also be a great idea as social connection is really important (read on!), as well as the physical benefits of moving your body.

SOCIAL CONNECTION

Humans are social beings – we are designed to connect with others and be part of a community. We may all have different-sized social groups or communities, but social connection is a really important part of survival. Connecting with others helps to develop our skills, understanding and knowledge, and helps us to feel good! Often when we feel sad, we can find ourselves doing fewer social things and then having less connection with other people. This can be due to lots of different reasons, including unhelpful thinking, low motivation or feelings of worry getting in the way. What we know, however, is if we push ourselves or plan (for example, using an activity timetable) to speak to or spend time with someone we trust and who usually helps us to feel good, then it will help to improve our mood. They might help distract us from our difficult thoughts or feelings, problem-solve or motivate us to do other things that help boost our mood. Sometimes, just sharing our difficult emotions with someone else can help make those feelings a little smaller and less overwhelming (see the **SAY HOW YOU FEEL** section on page 101 for more information).

THIS FEELING WON'T LAST FOR EVER.

POSITIVE SELF-TALK

Do you remember the **GLOOMY GOGGLES** we talked about earlier? These goggles can make the way your mind thinks when you are feeling sad become really negative. If you can, try to notice what your thoughts are when you are feeling really sad **(OR EVEN WHEN YOU ARE FEELING WORRIED – THIS WORKS FOR BOTH!)**. You might notice that certain thoughts or ideas keep coming up. Take some time to try to think of how you could argue with this thought – how could you turn it into a positive?

Once you have written down some ideas, practise saying these positive thoughts to yourself whenever you notice the negative thought comes up. The more you practise, the easier it will be for your brain to produce something positive when your difficult feelings are stronger. Try to follow these steps when you notice you are feeling sad or worried:

1 Notice you are having a negative thought – recognize it and decide to try to tackle it.

2 Think of all the reasons why this thought is not true or how it is unhelpful.

3 Use positive self-talk to turn the negative thought into a positive for example:

- "AS LONG AS I STAY CALM, I AM IN CONTROL."
- "IT IS THE [INSERT EMOTION HERE, FOR EXAMPLE, SADNESS OR WORRY] MAKING ME THINK IN THIS WAY, IT IS NOT THE TRUTH."
- "THIS FEELING WON'T LAST FOR EVER."
- "EVERYONE FEELS LIKE THIS SOMETIMES."
- "I AM SAFE."

NOTICE THREE POSITIVES IN YOUR DAY, EVERY DAY!

The **GLOOMY GOGGLES** that we can end up wearing when we feel sad can be really hard to take off! One really helpful way of keeping off the goggles is by practising noticing the positive things that have happened to you and around you.

Try to notice **THREE** things every day that went well, were positive, felt kind or helped you feel good **(EVEN IF IT WAS JUST A LITTLE BIT, OR FOR A SHORT TIME)**. Write these down, or even find someone you trust to share them with. They can share their own positive things with you. If this feels tricky to start with, you could try noticing three positive things for each other. They don't have to be big things – the little things are just as important. Maybe someone said hello and waved to you from across the playground, or someone held a door open for you or gave you one of their snacks? Perhaps you received a text message from someone you haven't heard from in a while, or maybe your parents made your favourite dinner?

JOYFUL JOURNAL

Do you remember before when we explained that when we feel sad, our thoughts change? One of the ways our thoughts change when we feel sad is that we can become unkind towards ourselves – this can be called **"SELF-CRITICAL"** or putting ourselves down. This keeps the sad feeling going and can even start affecting our self-esteem and confidence. Try keeping a special **NOTEBOOK**, where you can write down all the kind, nice and positive things people have said to you, and also make a note of all the moments you have achieved something or felt proud of yourself. The process of writing these down helps us to notice our own strengths and skills, which is really important for positive self-esteem and confidence (see below). It also helps us to see all the positives, which as we have explained, can be more difficult to see when we are wearing our **GLOOMY GOGGLES** of sadness.

NOTICING STRENGTHS

Noticing our strengths can help us feel good about ourselves, reduce sadness and build self-esteem. Our strengths can be things we do well, how we behave towards others (being kind, supportive or thoughtful) or characteristics that help us to manage the ups and the downs. These characteristics might be things like having courage, resilience or being very determined. Sometimes our strengths can be difficult to notice, especially if we are feeling sad or our thoughts have become unkind or self-critical. Thinking about times when you have achieved something, worked hard at something, helped another person or coped with something difficult can help to spot your strengths.

It's important to notice our own strengths. Having others point them out to us will not help us feel good if we can't notice them ourselves. However, having positive feedback from people we trust and who are important to us can be really powerful, especially when we've been feeling sad or have been hard on ourselves. Others who know us well can see things in us that we might not. Hearing positive feedback about something we have done well, ways in which others have appreciated us, or what they have noticed in us is really important. It helps us feel better connected to others, but also helps us look for and understand our own strengths.

It can sometimes feel difficult to notice or take on board the positive things other people say to us or notice us doing, especially if we have been feeling sad for a long time, or very often. If this is something you experience, it might take some practice to accept somebody saying something nice about you, or believe in your own strengths.

Take a few minutes to write down some of your strengths. Try to think of these in different categories: "SKILLS OR THINGS I AM GOOD AT", "HOW I BEHAVE OR INTERACT WITH OTHERS", "CHARACTERISTICS OR VALUES THAT HELP ME LEAD A POSITIVE LIFE" and finally "HOW DO I COPE WITH CHALLENGES – WHAT STRENGTHS DO I HAVE TO HELP WITH THIS?"

Once you have done this, ask friends or family members that you trust to write down three strengths they notice in you (you can share the suggestions above with them, if you like). Do any match with what you had written down or are they different?

Reminding yourself of your strengths at times when you are feeling sad, self-critical or as if things are not going well can really help you to move towards feeling good again.

FEELING ANGRY

As you are getting older, you will have all sorts to deal with, including the changes in your body and brain. Remember on page 10 we talked about how different parts of the brain mature (or "grow up") earlier than others? You might remember that the very last bit to develop is the front part of your brain, which helps you to think about what you do just before going ahead and doing it (it controls your impulses), and also manages and controls your emotions. This is partly why teenagers and young people can find they have **MOOD SWINGS** – another name for your emotions being very up and down. You might find that you are calm one moment and angry the next, or even that you react in a more emotional way than you used to. A bit like feeling sad or worried, feeling angry is completely normal. You shouldn't necessarily try to stop yourself feeling angry, but try to find safe ways to express it.

HERE ARE SOME OTHER WORDS YOU MIGHT USE TO DESCRIBE FEELING ANGRY:

IRRITABLE   FRUSTRATED

GRUMPY   OUTRAGED   FURIOUS

ANNOYED   LIVID   FUMING

JUST LIKE WHEN WE FEEL SAD OR WORRIED, FEELING ANGRY CAN ALSO
COME WITH FEELINGS IN OUR BODY. HERE ARE A FEW EXAMPLES:

- Feeling hot.
- Feeling your muscles tense up.
- Feeling restless or fidgety or like you can't stay still.
- Sweating.
- Feeling your skin tingling.
- Feeling your breathing or heart rate increase, sometimes you might feel as though you can hear your heart beating in your ears!
- Clenching (squeezing) your teeth together or your hands into fists.

HOW DOES ANGER FEEL?

Can you think of a time that you felt angry? What was happening to you when you felt like that? Where did you feel it in your body (trace and label the diagram on the next page)? Did you feel any other emotions at the same time?

READY FOR A FIGHT

We have already talked about the **FIGHT, FLIGHT** or **FREEZE** response, what it means and how it might feel. (If you need a refresher, turn back to page 19.) Well, anger is part of the **FIGHT** or **FLIGHT** response, just like feeling anxious or worried is. If you think about it – anger is really the **"FIGHT"** part of **FIGHT** or **FLIGHT**! You might feel angry if you think there is a threat or danger. This could include a threat of physical harm or injury, a threat to someone you care about, a threat to an item that is yours, or even a threat to your emotions or wellbeing. Any of these things could very reasonably trigger you to feel angry.

Remember we talked before about the stress hormone you release, adrenaline? It is a rush of adrenaline that causes these unpleasant physical symptoms, and both anger and anxiety can make this happen – so the symptoms of both can be similar. Let's remind ourselves of some of the feelings you might experience when you are angry or anxious. Not everyone feels all of the symptoms in the same way, but these are some examples that lots of people describe:

PHYSICAL SENSATION	ANGER	ANXIETY
FEELING SWEATY	✓	✓
FEELING YOUR HEART RACING	✓	✓
FEELING YOUR BREATHING GETTING QUICKER	✓	✓
FEELING HOT	✓	✓
FEELING TINGLY	✓	✓
MUSCLE TENSION	✓	✓

IF YOU DREW A BODY MAP FOR ANGER OR WORRY, GO BACK AND LOOK AT IT – SEE IF YOU FELT ANY OF THESE SENSATIONS.

As we said before, **FIGHT**, **FLIGHT** or **FREEZE** mode pretty much bypasses any sensible thoughts we might have about the situation. Our body just automatically gets us ready to attack or run away! This can make it really hard to see things clearly. Of course, while this is very helpful when we are in a truly life-threatening situation **(LIKE BEING ATTACKED BY A SABRE-TOOTHED TIGER)**, it is less helpful when it is triggered by everyday life. Let's face it, most situations where we feel angry are not life-threatening.

As we go through life and experience more of these situations we can begin to recognize when we might need to respond in an angry way, or when we might be able to handle things in a calmer or more thoughtful way. As we grow and learn, we will begin to notice when our **FIGHT**, **FLIGHT** or **FREEZE** response is being activated, and how we can perhaps respond differently.

ASK DR EMILY

Q: What makes us feel angry?

A: We will all have different triggers that cause us to feel different emotions. We can feel angry when we have been treated unfairly by other people, or we notice unfairness around us, or perhaps when we face difficult experiences.

Most often, we experience anger when we are really feeling other emotions underneath. This is why anger is sometimes described as a secondary emotion. It can act like a mask for other difficult feelings, such as sadness, worry, shame or disappointment. As we've already talked about, anger is part of our **FIGHT** or **FLIGHT** response. This means it often pops up straight away in a certain situation, before we can stop and think how someone or something has really made us feel. Being angry might feel easier than trying to work out and deal with the feelings underneath. The problem with this is that once the angry feeling has settled, we can still be left with the feelings that led us to feel angry in the first place.

When we feel angry, we can say things that we don't really mean or that hurt others. We can act differently to usual, or sometimes the angry feeling might lead us to shout, scream or lash out aggressively. Once the anger has passed, thinking about how we behaved or the things we said while angry can leave us feeling other emotions including sadness, regret or worry.

It is really important to try to stop and think about what is causing you to feel angry and whether there are other feelings that might be contributing to this.

ANGRY THOUGHTS

As we have already heard, when we feel angry the way we think can change. We often find it difficult to think clearly and rationalize our thoughts. Sometimes, people describe a "RED MIST" or "SEEING RED" when they feel angry. They describe this as a kind of barrier that comes over their mind and makes it difficult to see the situation as it really is or think clearly.

Experiencing strong emotions can make the communication in the brain more difficult and leave us less able to think clearly. Just like when we feel worried or sad, there are some really common ways of unhelpful thinking that we can all find ourselves falling into when we feel angry. If we notice when we are thinking in these ways, then it is easier to stop and try to change and take control over the way we feel.

UNHELPFUL WORDS

The words we tend to use to describe our experiences, situations or our judgements about other people and interactions, can be unhelpful when we are experiencing anger. We can use words that are more negative than positive when we feel let down or that something has been unfair. When we feel angry, we are more likely to use unhelpful, negative labels for other people or situations. Sometimes this can include being **RUDE** or using **UNKIND** or **SPITEFUL** words.

OVERGENERALIZATION

This is something our thoughts can do whenever we feel any strong emotion. **OVERGENERALIZATION** means that we can start to apply our experience of one single event or interaction to every event or interaction that might be similar. For example, we might say: **"THINGS NEVER GO TO PLAN"**, **"YOU ALWAYS DO THAT"**, **"NOBODY KNOWS HOW TO DO THAT"** or **"NOBODY UNDERSTANDS ME"**. This can stop us from noticing more positive experiences that could help us to change how we see the situation and reduce our angry feelings.

CLOUDED THOUGHTS

As we have learned from exploring the other emotions in this book, when experiencing a difficult emotion these feelings can affect how we see situations. When we experience anger, we can often misread situations – for example, we might think someone is doing something deliberately to annoy us, when in actual fact it may have been an accident. We may also think that somebody planned to get a certain reaction out of us, when really we can't know that for sure, and it's probably our emotions and feelings making us think like that!

If we try to just look at the **FACTS** about a situation, rather than what our angry minds might be thinking about it, then it can help us to see things more clearly. We can start to work out what is really happening, rather than what our anger is trying to make us see.

IS IT ALL BAD?

A bit like feeling sad or worried, anger can sometimes be thought of as a **"NEGATIVE"** or unhelpful emotion. But everyone will feel all sorts of different emotions during their lives, and all are important in one way or another. Just like feeling sad or worried, feeling angry can also be helpful sometimes. Remember, anger is your body looking out for you or protecting you from something that it thinks might be harmful – just like feeling worried can be useful in some situations.

Feeling angry can make us notice that perhaps we are facing something unfair, or simply that something isn't quite right. Sometimes when we feel angry it can then make us feel **MOTIVATED**. For example, if you are faced with a situation that you don't like and it makes you angry, you might begin to think of the ways that you can handle that situation to make it better. In this way, anger can push us towards our goals, to help us achieve things. Perhaps you have heard of someone called Greta Thunberg? When she was a teenager she began to campaign to protect the environment, and she is now known all over the world for the work she has done. This might have started with Greta feeling upset or angry about pollution or the effect that humans are having on Earth – but she turned this into something positive by **MOTIVATING** herself to push for change.

Anger might also help us in our relationships with others – if something makes you angry, you can talk to others and work through it together, explaining your feelings and why you are upset, which could make your relationship with that person better.

So, feeling angry is a normal emotion. In the right situations, anger can be helpful by helping us notice when things are unfair or not right, and by pushing us to try to fix things or change those situations for the better. This helps us protect ourselves and move forwards positively in our lives.

ASK DR EMILY

Q: What if I feel angry a lot?

A: We have said that experiencing anger is normal, and not to think of it as a negative emotion, that it can even be helpful. But a bit like feeling very worried or very sad, feeling very angry can also be unhelpful sometimes. If you find that you are feeling angry a lot of the time, it may be time to think about getting a bit of advice. Sometimes when people feel very angry it can make them act in a physically aggressive way, like breaking things, or even physically hitting or hurting other people or themselves. Other things to look out for are if your feelings of anger are getting you in trouble at school or at home, if they are stopping you from being able to have positive relationships with your friends or family, or just generally stopping you being able to live your life in the way that you want. If any of this sounds familiar, or if you notice that you are starting to express your anger in an unhelpful way, speak to an adult you trust to get some support.

If you are feeling angry a lot of the time, it is important to think about what other feelings you might be experiencing. As we have talked about, anger very rarely comes to visit on its own and is often a secondary emotion. It is possible that you might be feeling worried or sad about things too. Sometimes if we haven't noticed these emotions, it can present as anger.

HOW TO MANAGE ANGER

There are lots of helpful ways you can manage your feelings of anger, so let's have a think about some of these.

As anger is part of our **FIGHT** or **FLIGHT** response, it can be difficult to stop and think things through before we respond to the feeling. With practice, however, we can learn to take more control over how we immediately respond to our angry feelings.

COUNTING TO TEN

One of the simplest things to do when you begin to feel angry is to count to ten slowly while trying to practise some controlled breathing (see below). Counting to ten gives a bit of space between what has made you feel angry and how you are expressing your angry feeling. This gives enough time to try to help you to think clearly about what the most helpful way of responding could be. It helps to push down the feeling of wanting to respond in a quick or aggressive way.

CONTROLLED BREATHING

One of the most helpful ways to manage anger is to **BREATHE!** Breathing helps us feel calm and relaxed and gives the brain something to focus on while we are waiting for our immediate anger to settle. Whilst you are pausing and counting to ten, try to practise some controlled breathing.

Why not try the **SQUARE BREATHING** or **FIVE-FINGER BREATHING** exercises on page 59? These can be just as good for anger as for anxiety, because they help you stay calm and focused while the surge in your adrenaline levels is passing.

DOING SOMETHING PHYSICAL

The way our bodies feel when we experience anger can mean that we often need to do something physical to get rid of the built-up tension, adrenaline and stress in our bodies. Try the following ideas to see if they help to reduce your angry feelings:

- Go outside and shout really loudly.
- Use a stress ball:

  …squeeze it in each of your hands, ten times, really quickly.

  …squeeze it tightly for as long as possible with each hand.

  …throw it really hard against a wall.
- Scrunch or rip up paper.
- Scribble really hard on a piece of paper with a pencil.
- Squeeze or hit a soft pillow.

MARTIAL ARTS

Joining a martial arts class or club can be a really helpful way to manage anger (AND OTHER EMOTIONS!) more positively. Martial arts such as Kung Fu and Jiu-Jitsu combine lots of the strategies we have already talked about in this book, and can help you to learn to use these skills to channel your energy and feelings into helpful responses that boost your sense of self-control. The benefits of martial arts include:

- Getting your body moving and releasing endorphins.
- Helping you to think mindfully and focus your attention on something other than what has led you to feel angry.
- Helping you develop controlled breathing. Different

martial arts teach different breathing techniques, but all help you to learn to breathe in a calm and controlled way.

STOPP!

The STOPP technique is really helpful in managing angry feelings, but also works well for other emotions too. Practise the steps below in order every time you notice feeling a strong emotion, like anger.

Stop – pause for a moment, count to ten

Take a breath – practise controlled breathing, breathe in through your nose and out through your mouth. **TOP TIP: YOU COULD TRY USING SQUARE BREATHING OR FIVE-FINGER BREATHING HERE**.

Observe – notice what thoughts are going through your mind. What do you notice in your body? What is it that has led to you feel this way?

Perspective – try to think about the bigger picture. Take a step back and think about how you could look at the situation in a different way. What might you say to a friend if they were in the same situation?

Proceed – practise the strategies you have learned that help you with this feeling. What would be the most helpful thing to do right now? Where else can you focus your attention?

ANGER VOLCANO

Different strategies will work more or less well depending on the level of anger you're feeling. Try drawing the volcano on the next page to think about the times and things that make you feel angry (the trigger), and how strongly you felt at the time. Next to each level of the volcano, write a strategy you think you will find helpful to manage it.

EXPLODING

BUBBLING UP

RUMBLING

OK

GREAT

Most people will find that when they experience strong angry feelings **(AS IF THE VOLCANO IS ERUPTING)**, they need to use certain strategies first, such as counting or controlled breathing, before looking at it a different way or challenging unhelpful thinking. Over time you will be able to know which strategies help prevent your angry feelings from getting worse, and you can put these lower down on your volcano. **TAKE ANOTHER LOOK AT YOUR VOLCANO AND THE TRIGGERS YOU HAVE DESCRIBED.** What other emotions might these triggers be leading you to feel?

UNHELPFUL STRATEGIES

Coping with difficult emotions is not easy. Sometimes we can end up using strategies that might seem like they could help or make us feel better for a short time, but in the long term become unhelpful. It might cause you or other people pain or upset, affect your physical health, or stop you from doing things that are important to you. Anything that could make you unsafe is not a helpful way of coping.

When we are finding it hard to manage difficult emotions, we can feel unsettled and as if things are out of our control. We might then try to seek control over the things that we can. Some people might start trying to control whether to do or not do certain things, such as their usual activities, or they might begin to control other things in their life like the types or amounts of food that they eat. If you notice you have lost your appetite for a long period of time or are worried about changes in your weight, speak to a grown-up.

Sometimes when it feels difficult to manage our emotions for a long period of time, we can feel **STUCK**. It can be difficult to know how to make a positive change. At these times, we can have thoughts of wanting to hurt ourselves and sometimes we can act upon these thoughts. Hurting yourself might seem like it could provide a short-term distraction from the difficult emotion, or it might provide a sense of control. But what we know is that distraction or feeling better doesn't last very long. Often the thing that caused you to feel that way is still there. If anything, it can often be stronger, especially if you also then feel worried about hurting yourself. Stopping having thoughts of hurting yourself is not always easy, but it is a **REALLY IMPORTANT THING** to learn to do in order to help **KEEP YOU SAFE** and find **POSITIVE, LONGER-LASTING WAYS OF COPING**. The most important thing to do if you notice these thoughts, or if you have hurt yourself deliberately, is to speak to someone you trust. They can help you find further support.

If any of this feels familiar to you, or you think you might be using some of these unhelpful strategies, try not to worry. Developing unhelpful strategies is not something you have chosen to do, they usually develop over time from having to deal with difficult emotions. It is important, however, that you speak to someone and seek support. There are lots of people who can help you think about other ways to cope and places you can go to for extra support, in order to keep you safe and healthy (see the **SEEKING MORE SUPPORT** section on page 125). Practising the other strategies we have talked about in this book will also help.

SAY HOW YOU FEEL

Communicating how we feel is really important. It can help us to recognize what it is that we are feeling, what might have led us to feel that way, and help us feel less alone. Sharing our thoughts and feelings with someone we trust can help us to problem-solve and think of different ways to help manage what is going on and deal with the difficult emotion. You might share how you are feeling with a friend you trust, a relative or even a teacher. Whoever you choose to share your emotions with, it is important that you trust them, and they are able to listen to what you have to say and are supportive of you.

To begin with, it might feel a little strange talking about how you feel to other people, but it is a really **HEALTHY** thing to do! Try some of the ideas on the next page – they might help you to feel more confident when sharing your emotions.

Arrange a time and space to talk to someone you trust about any worries or difficult feelings you may have. You could do this every week, for example, or arrange a set time. Make sure to remove any distractions (like **TV, MOBILE PHONES, OTHER TASKS**) during these conversations so you can really concentrate and listen to each other.

Try not to talk about worries or difficult feelings right before going to bed. Often things can feel more worrying at night. It might be helpful to keep a pen and paper by your bed so you can write down worries that come to mind before bed. You can then plan a time to discuss these worries the next day.

IF YOU FIND TALKING ABOUT FEELINGS DIFFICULT, YOU COULD TRY COMMUNICATING IN DIFFERENT WAYS:

- Write your thoughts and feelings in a diary.
- Draw a picture to represent your feelings or what is bothering you.
- Use a traffic-light system to explain how you are feeling to others. For example, you could let the people who care about you know how you are feeling by texting them a coloured circle. A **RED** circle could mean that you are finding things difficult, or feeling very sad or worried and need support. **YELLOW** could mean you are having some difficult feelings, but are managing these, although some support might be helpful. **GREEN** could mean you are feeling good with no big worries. You can make a plan together to agree what each colour will mean and how best to support each colour.

If talking to someone you know feels too difficult, you can speak with a professional (someone whose job it is to support people with their mental health) on the helplines and textlines at the end of this book (see **SEEKING MORE SUPPORT** on page 125).

ASK DR EMILY

Q: What do I do if a friend talks to me about their mental health?

A: The most important thing to do if someone speaks to you about how they are feeling, or something they are finding difficult, is to listen. Knowing that someone else has heard what they are feeling or finding difficult can help them to feel less lonely, increase their feeling of being supported and help them to think more clearly. People used to say, **"A PROBLEM SHARED IS A PROBLEM HALVED,"** and that is definitely true.

Your job is not to fix the challenge they are experiencing, but to let them know you will support them in finding the help they need to make things feel easier. You might have some ideas to share, or can help them to problem-solve, but it is also OK if you don't or can't solve the difficulty. Being there for someone and offering your support and kindness is just as important. You can also help your friend by distracting them with other things to focus on, helping them to relax, doing activities they usually enjoy and helping them to think about their self-care or things that make them feel good.

If you are worried about your friend, if they are finding it difficult to cope or you are worried about keeping them safe, it is important to speak to a trusted adult. It is important to do this even if your friend says they don't want this. The adult will help you and your friend to think about other ways of seeking the support they might need.

MIND-BODY LINK

We have already explained that our mind and our body are closely linked, with the health of one directly affecting the other. This is why it is really important to look after your physical health, as well as your emotional health, to keep you feeling good. If you think back to the very beginning of this book, we spent some time understanding emotions and how these affect our physical feelings in our bodies. Sometimes we can experience physical pain when we experience different emotions. This pain is very real, but is triggered by a change in our emotions. For example, many people can experience headaches when they are feeling worried or sad. This headache is because the emotion is driving a response in your body, rather than there being a problem in your head. In exactly the same way, suffering from physical health problems can affect our mental health – for example, children or adults with a serious health condition may feel stressed or show anxiety symptoms because of their worry about their illness.

GUT-BRAIN AXIS

Your brain and gut are directly connected. They are always

working together to keep the body going and to share information about thoughts and feelings. If one is happy, then the other will be too. In the same way, if one is unhappy then the other will also be unhappy. You might have noticed "butterflies" in your stomach when you have felt nervous, or described something as "gut-wrenching" when you have felt worried or scared. You might have experienced needing the toilet urgently when you have felt worried, or that thinking about food can trigger you to feel hungry **(BECAUSE IT RELEASES STOMACH JUICES!)**.

Tummy aches are another really common symptom that people can experience when they are feeling worried, stressed or sad. For example, if you are feeling worried about a test, you might experience stomach pain. In this case, the pain does not mean there is a physical problem or infection in your stomach, but it is the worry which has triggered a physical feeling in your body.

Because of the way the gut and the brain are connected, if you are someone who notices frequent tummy pain or difficulties with going to the toilet, you may find that using different coping strategies to deal with your worries, stress or sadness can help improve these symptoms too. **BUT OF COURSE, IF YOU ARE FEELING ANY PHYSICAL OR MENTAL HEALTH PROBLEMS, IT'S ALWAYS A GOOD IDEA TO TALK TO AN ADULT YOU TRUST OR YOUR DOCTOR.**

This connection works in the other direction too. If we look after our gut by feeding it the right foods, water and nutrients, it can have a direct impact on our mood and help us feel good!

EMBRACING CHANGE

One important thing to mention is how **TRANSITIONS** in life can sometimes make things feel a little difficult. Transition basically means change, or moving from one thing to another. Examples of transitions we might experience are moving school, moving house, a new addition to the family (like a younger brother or sister), changes within your family, or even falling out with friends. Most people in the world find transitions difficult – even adults! This is because humans generally like things to be predictable (to know what's coming up) and consistent (things staying the same). Sometimes, if a transition is coming up, we might even try to avoid it! This is all because our brains can just find it difficult or even overwhelming to experience change.

As much as change can be difficult, it is part of life. Things end, and new things start. We all leave primary school and go to secondary school, we all go through puberty, we all leave school one day and start a job or go to university. One day, you'll probably even move out of home and live away from your family. These are all transitions. As we get older, transitions can get bigger and may be trickier to handle. That's why it's so important to get used to handling change while growing up, in preparation for being a successful and happy grown-up!

HERE ARE MY TOP TIPS FOR MANAGING CHANGES, BIG OR SMALL:

1 If a change is coming, it can be easier to manage if you plan ahead to get your head around what might happen. This allows you time to process and prepare as best as you can.

2 Keeping your usual routine can help make things feel more familiar and predictable. Even if some things are changing, try to keep some the same to make life feel more manageable.

3 Don't worry if changes feel hard! Understanding your feelings and saying when things are tricky can be helpful. It's totally normal and you can be sure that if you're finding it hard, someone else is too.

4 Talk to others. A problem shared is a problem halved! Just like other difficult situations, talking to somebody can make it feel easier. It could be a friend or family member, or someone you trust and you know is a good listener.

5 Don't forget to have fun! Sometimes when it's a stressful time we can forget to enjoy ourselves. Doing a fun activity can help distract us for a while and keep our mood positive.

BOOST YOUR SELF-ESTEEM

You may remember the words **"SELF-ESTEEM"** we mentioned earlier. It might be helpful to talk a little more about it and how we can make our own as good as possible. As a reminder, self-esteem means how we feel about ourselves – specifically feeling positive. People with good self-esteem feel proud of their achievements, feel that others accept them for who they are, and believe in themselves. Flip this the other way around – people whose self-esteem isn't great often feel they aren't good enough, doubt themselves or are very harsh on themselves.

So how can we build our own self-esteem? There is no right or wrong answer to this question, as everyone will feel slightly differently about themselves. A good place to start is by being positive about yourself in **YOUR OWN** head. Self-esteem really comes from within. Although it is helpful to hear others saying nice things about you (and as you will read in the next chapter, having friends around you who are supportive and positive definitely helps) – the most important person who can build your self-esteem is **YOU!** Just thinking in positive and understanding ways about yourself is a great start. For example, say you lost a football match or didn't do very well in your maths homework – try to think **"IT'S OK – I DID MY BEST AND I'LL KEEP TRYING"** or **"WE DIDN'T WIN BUT I HAD LOADS OF FUN!"** If you think things like **"I'M RUBBISH AT FOOTBALL"** or **"I ALWAYS DO BADLY IN MATHS ... WHAT'S THE POINT?"** then next time you will be more likely to feel negatively again, maybe before you even start! If you keep thinking in negative ways, in time you might start to notice your self-esteem isn't great in other areas of your life. It just feels miserable and makes you sad – so focus on building your self-esteem.

Another important thing to remember about self-esteem is that no one is good at everything. It's easy to feel like everything we do needs to be exactly right – but that's not the case. No one is perfect. Everybody in the whole world has things that they are good at, and things that they aren't so great at. Think of Usain Bolt. He is an amazing runner, and has smashed world records. But if you put him in his country's Olympic hockey team, he probably wouldn't be the best player! It's very easy to be critical of yourself, without remembering the things at which you are amazing. Everyone has strengths and weaknesses, it's just about noticing when you do well at something and forgiving yourself when things don't go to plan. This helps us to develop the things that we want to improve, rather than just giving up. Remember when you start a new skill, you will never be good at it straight away. Taking the time to learn new things and seeing yourself improve over time is good for your self-esteem and for **BUILDING RESILIENCE** (like we talked about on pages 71–72).

Another way you can boost your self-esteem is by setting goals for things you would like to improve and working towards them. Let's imagine someone trying to learn a new language (I find this really difficult, so I am using it as an example!). They might decide to start off by learning some new words for 15 minutes each day. Then as they know more words, they would start putting sentences together, or even trying to speak to someone else in that language. Setting manageable goals for yourself, trying to stick to them and then being proud of yourself afterwards is a great way to build your self-esteem. Also, focusing on the things that have gone well instead of the things that have not gone so well will really help. Let's say you've had a hard day at school … it's OK to acknowledge that the day was hard, but perhaps try thinking something like, **"MY LESSONS WERE REALLY TOUGH TODAY, BUT I REALLY ENJOYED PLAYING AT LUNCHTIME WITH MY FRIENDS!"**

BEST-OF-ME BRAINSTORM

A top tip for building self-esteem is to think of all the things you are good at, or positive things you could say about yourself.

Try to write these things down in a list. Writing down things that you are good at can feel a bit funny at first, but it feels great after! Then, if you are having a day when you are feeling worried or are doubting yourself, read your list again to remind yourself of your amazing strengths and try to focus on those.

The final thing I wanted to say about self-esteem is that while we are building our own self-esteem (and self-esteem comes from within ourselves), remember to be kind and encouraging to those around us. Everyone will be worrying about their own challenges or difficulties, and sometimes a kind or encouraging word from a friend can make all the difference. Just as you will take positive things from others – try to be positive back. Also, helping others is a really positive experience that can make you feel great about yourself, building your own self-esteem as well as theirs! By helping each other, we can all build our self-esteem together.

YOUR SUPPORT TEAM

When we are focusing on our mental health, it's really important to think about the people around you and those who support you in your life. Think of some of the people who are important to you: your family, friends, teammates or neighbours. Generally speaking, it is a good idea to surround yourself with people who make you happy! Friends will come and go in life, but a good friend won't judge you, and will like you for who you are – exactly as you are. But how can you tell if someone is a good person to hang out with or not? Let's have a think about some of the ways you can recognize a positive and healthy friendship…

1   An important thing to look for in a friend is being **KIND**. This means being caring, being respectful, looking out for you, understanding where you are coming from, listening to you and generally being there for you in good times or bad. Being kind also means that they understand when you are upset and comfort you. It is also important that your friend understands and accepts your beliefs and opinions, even if they perhaps have different ones.

2   A friend should be **TRUSTWORTHY**. This is a long word that basically means you can trust them. This usually means that they are **HONEST** (tell you the truth). It also means that you can rely on them when you need them – for example, if you are having a difficult day knowing that they will take time to listen and help you.

3   How about being **FUN?** As we have already mentioned, you won't feel like having fun all the time **(AND IT IS IMPORTANT THAT YOUR FRIENDS STICK AROUND WHEN YOU AREN'T IN THE MOOD)**, but having fun together is a great thing in a friendship! Those fun experiences can bond you together as friends.

Don't forget, while these are all things you might look out for in a friend, your friends deserve to have those things in return from you. That's another important part of a friendship, it should be fair and equal – or **"GIVE AND TAKE"**. In other words, it's not fair if you are kind and supportive to your friend but they don't listen to you, or they are unkind to you, or vice versa. You might have heard of the saying **"TREAT OTHER PEOPLE**

AS YOU WOULD LIKE TO BE TREATED". This is a **CRUCIAL** part of a healthy and happy friendship. So, make sure you try to be all of the things on this list to your friends and hopefully you will create a positive and supportive friendship between you.

Not only that, it's important to remember that a real friend is not someone who just tells you that you are amazing the whole time, and lets you get your own way. They should be someone who cares for you, understands you, and is an equal person in the friendship. This might mean that you sometimes disagree with each other's opinions, but you can still discuss things in a supportive and respectful way. Even if you make a huge mistake, a true friend will talk about it, forgive you, and get back on track with your friendship.

FRIEND OR FRENEMY?

Remember, we are all allowed to have a bad day – for example, your friend might be a bit grumpy with you one day and you might think it is unfair. But if you notice that a friend is often quite grumpy, or even unkind to you, then it might be time to think about whether the friendship is making you happy or not. Let's have a think about some things you could look out for if you are worried that someone you think is a friend is making things hard for you:

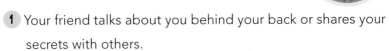

1 Your friend talks about you behind your back or shares your secrets with others.

2 They might pressure you into doing things that you don't

want to do, or into making bad decisions.

3 If they judge you, question you or make you feel bad about yourself.

4 They aren't around for you when you need help or advice.

5 They might try to take advantage of you, and only talk to you when they want something from you.

6 They make you feel sad when you spend time with them, rather than happy and energized.

7 They leave you out in group situations.

HOPEFULLY YOU WON'T EXPERIENCE THINGS LIKE THIS IN YOUR FRIENDSHIPS, BUT WHAT SHOULD YOU DO IF YOUR FRIEND IS DOING SOME OF THESE THINGS? HERE ARE MY TOP TIPS FOR WHAT TO DO WHEN YOU HAVE A DIFFICULT FRIENDSHIP:

1 Talk to someone else about it. I have already mentioned the saying "a problem shared is a problem halved"! I really think this is true – in other words, when you speak to someone else, it can really make your problem feel like something you can handle. This might be with another friend, a parent, teacher, brother, sister or an adult you trust.

2 Try not to blame yourself. When you have friendship difficulties, it can feel like it is all your fault. While it is important to think about the things you could do differently, it is never completely one person's fault, including yours.

3 Don't try to change to suit someone else. Remember – you are who you are! If a friend doesn't like that, or if you feel pressured to change yourself in one way or another, then

they aren't the friend for you. It might feel super important to act the same way as someone else, or try to blend in with the group, but remember, individuality is a gift! If you love and appreciate all the things about you that make you different, other people will too.

FALLING-OUT

Sometimes, we can try to work things out with a friend we have fallen out with. That usually involves chatting with each other about what has made you feel upset or has made the friendship not so great. Remember to **LISTEN** to your friend and hear their point of view, but also make sure they listen to you. If this doesn't help and the friendship just isn't working, sometimes we have to make the decision to end a friendship. This can feel like a really difficult thing to do, and it is a really brave step. Sometimes when you end a friendship it can make the other person upset, or even unkind. If you experience this, or if you think you are being bullied, speak to a teacher or another adult to get some help. If you are thinking about ending a friendship, you might start to think about other people in your life that you could be friends with. Have a think if you know anyone with the qualities we talked about earlier **(KIND, TRUSTWORTHY, FUN)** – perhaps you already have another person in your life with these qualities that you can build a friendship with? Sometimes, a great friend is already in our lives and we just need to notice and appreciate them. Sometimes a great friend can be a family member – like a brother or sister, or a cousin – think about who you might have in your friendship circle. You might have many or just a few – either way, it's the quality and strength of the friendships that are important.

WE ARE ALL DIFFERENT

We've touched on this already, but I wanted to talk a little bit about how important it is to be understanding and accepting of the differences between you and others. This might be the way that you look or dress, or your culture, religion or beliefs, or even the things that you like to do. For example, some people have different colour skin, hair or eyes, or perhaps they are taller, shorter, bigger or smaller. Everyone likes different things, whether that is food, activities or clothes. A bit like we have mentioned with friendships – it is really important to **TREAT OTHER PEOPLE AS YOU WOULD LIKE TO BE TREATED.** So if you want people to be accepting and understanding about your appearance or beliefs, try to understand other people's. **THERE IS NO RIGHT OR WRONG WAY TO LOOK, THINK OR FEEL,** and the more we understand and accept the differences between us and others, the more our world will be a better and happier place! Sometimes it can take time or be difficult to understand someone else's differences, but we can still try our hardest to be respectful of them.

It's really important to understand that just like we accept others' physical appearances, we need to learn to understand that our brains can all work differently too. Some people might find that **NEURODIVERSITY** (the way their brains work), can make some things feel more difficult to cope with. We all need to be supportive of each other, and understand that some of us may need a few adjustments to make things feel more manageable. That might be things like needing a bit more time to complete schoolwork, requiring a quiet and calm environment, needing breaks from learning or extra support at school. Just remember – we are all special and unique.

IF WE WERE ALL THE SAME, THE WORLD WOULD BE A PRETTY BORING PLACE! ALL OF THIS COMES BACK TO "TREATING OTHERS AS YOU WOULD LIKE TO BE TREATED". THAT IS ONE OF THE MOST IMPORTANT MESSAGES TO TAKE HOME FROM THIS BOOK.

BULLYING

So, we have thought about how you might experience a positive friendship, and perhaps what you might notice if a friendship isn't so great. But what about if you are worried that you are being bullied?

Bullying can mean all sorts of things, but it is basically any behaviour that hurts someone else, whether that is **PHYSICAL** (like hitting or pushing someone) or **EMOTIONAL** (like being unkind or name-calling).

Bullying can happen over a long period of time, where perhaps you don't notice it at first, but then over time you might start to feel more worried or upset about it. It can sometimes feel difficult to know whether you are being bullied, so here are some examples of things to look out for:

- Being left out, feeling excluded or on your own.
- Being threatened – that means someone saying or doing something that makes you worried that they will try to harm you in some way.
- Being laughed at or made fun of.
- People talking nastily about you behind your back – even spreading rumours about you to others.
- People being generally unkind, this could include somebody being very critical of you a lot of the time, or using unkind words when talking to you.
- Physical bullying could include hitting, punching, kicking or slapping somebody, or taking or breaking your belongings.

These are all examples of bullying behaviour that could happen inside or outside of school. But you may have also heard of a new type of bullying that has started to happen over the last few years called cyberbullying. When I was at school, cyberbullying wasn't really a thing **(AND I'M NOT THAT OLD, I PROMISE!)**. That's probably because the internet wasn't used as much as it is now, and there weren't really any smartphones or social media. But now, most people are able to get online when they are at school or at home, and many people have smartphones and social media , even before the recommended age, which is usually 13. While this is great in lots of ways, as we can learn a lot from technology like the internet, it can have its downsides, and one of these is cyberbullying.

ASK DR EMILY

Q: What is cyberbullying?

A: Cyberbullying is basically any bullying that takes place online. That could include on a computer, laptop, games console, tablet or smartphone. Cyberbullying can include:

- Nasty or unkind text messages or messages on social media – this can sometimes be called **TROLLING**, which is when somebody sends unkind messages or comments to someone else with the purpose of upsetting them. These comments are often untrue.

- Someone sending photos or videos of you without your permission, trying to upset you. This might be something you find embarrassing.

- Setting up fake accounts online to be unkind or embarrass someone.

- Leaving someone out of a group, activity or game online.

- Pressuring someone to send photos or videos that they are not comfortable with.

- Pressuring someone to do things they don't want to do.

WHAT TO DO ABOUT BULLYING

If someone is behaving in a way that is making you feel sad, worried or uncomfortable, whether that is online or in person – that is **NOT OK**. If you are worried that you are being bullied, it is really important that you speak to someone about it. That could be a parent, teacher or another adult that you trust. They can help you understand a little more about what might be happening and what can be done to help. If the bullying is happening at school or online, it's often helpful that your teachers know about it so that they can help and support you. Or, if the bullying is happening at a club outside of school, your parents might want to speak to the person in charge there. Sometimes when you are being bullied you can feel embarrassed or ashamed that it is happening to you. It can even affect somebody's mental health, especially if it happens for a long time or is severe, which is why it is so important to get help early. Please don't feel ashamed or worried to speak to someone. Remember, if you are being bullied, it is not your fault at all. **YOU ARE AWESOME, LOVED AND VALUED!** Try to focus on the things that make you feel happy, the things you enjoy doing, and people who make you feel good about yourself.

SO WHAT NOW?

So, we have reached the end of this book. We have learnt about four important emotions – **FEELING GOOD**, **SAD**, **WORRIED** and **ANGRY**. Remember all of these emotions are completely normal, and we will all feel them at some time or other.

Sometimes, we can find one or more of these emotions a bit tricky to manage, but hopefully you have found some of the strategies we have talked about helpful. Perhaps in the future, if you find yourself feeling a bit sad, worried or angry, you could open this book and remind yourself of some of the hints and tips we talked about to try to make things feel a bit more manageable. You might find that one or two things work particularly well for you, so give them a go and see which you like.

Remember all of our brains work in their own amazing and unique way, so there is no right or wrong way to take care of yourself.

We've also talked a lot about the important links between your body and your mind, so looking after your physical and mental health go hand in hand. It's also super important to share your emotions with others, and in turn to be supportive and kind to your friends.

You might find that even after reading all of the information in this book that you still have some questions or worries. Don't forget, there are lots of places you can go for advice, I've included a list of people and organizations at the end of this book. You can always ask a grown-up you trust, too, as you will find that most of them have had their own experiences with managing tricky emotions when they were growing up. Never feel embarrassed to ask questions or talk about your mental health. The more we are all open and honest with each other, the more we will all feel supported to become the very best versions of ourselves. As you go through the journey from being a child to a grown-up, you will learn so much about yourself, and find your own special place in the world.

Remember – you are special and unique and the world is lucky to have you in it!

SEEKING MORE SUPPORT

Childline/NSPCC
Visit childline.org.uk or call 0800 1111

NHS Every Mind Matters
nhs.uk/every-mind-matters/mental-wellbeing-tips/youth-mental-health

Mind Charity
mind.org.uk/for-young-people/how-to-get-help-and-support/useful-contacts

Shout
Visit giveusashout.org or text SHOUT to 85258

Young Minds
Visit youngminds.org.uk or text YM to 85258

Better Sleep
bettersleep.com

Oxford Mindfulness Centre
oxfordmindfulness.org/learn-mindfulness/online-sessions-podcasts

Leaves in the Stream Exercise
mindfulnessmuse.com/wp-content/uploads/2011/09/Cognitive-Defusion-Exercise-1.pdf

Headspace
headspace.com

Mindful
mindful.org/category/meditation

Anxiety UK
anxietyuk.org.uk

Happy Maps
happymaps.co.uk

IF YOU REQUIRE URGENT SUPPORT OR YOU ARE CONCERNED ABOUT KEEPING YOURSELF SAFE, PLEASE CONTACT YOUR GP (DOCTOR) OR ATTEND A&E OR CALL 999.

You can also contact one of the following helplines, which provide urgent support:

Samaritans
Visit samaritans.org or call 116 123
Samaritans are available to call 24 hours a day, every day.

**Papyrus
(Prevention of Young Suicide)**
Call HOPELINE247 on 0800 068 4141 or text 07786 209 687. Lines are open 24 hours every day of the year.

GLOSSARY

Achievement The feeling when you complete something successfully or with skill.

Adrenaline A hormone that your body creates to help you react quickly in an exciting, stressful or dangerous situation.

Anxiety Feeling worried, scared, nervous or fearful.

Automatically Something that happens by itself, or without a person thinking/being aware of it.

Bullying Causing hurt or harm to someone else, either physically or emotionally.

Cyberbullying Any bullying that takes place online, either through phones, tablets or video games.

Catastrophizing When you think that the worst possible thing will definitely happen.

Consequences The results of behaving in a certain way or taking a specific action.

Emotions Another word for feelings (happy, sad, anger, love).

Fight, flight or freeze Your body's response to a dangerous or threatening situation.

Feelings Another word for emotions or the different physical sensations we can experience in our bodies.

Frontal lobe The part of the brain that helps you plan, make decisions and think about what may happen if you do something.

Gland An organ in the body which produces important chemicals or information that sends messages around the body.

Hormones Chemicals in your body that are like messengers, travelling around your body coordinating how your body develops and makes things work.

Mental health The health of your mind. How you think and feel about yourself, others and the world around you.

Motivation A process where you feel ready and keen to do an activity or reach a goal.

Overgeneralization Taking one experience and applying it to other situations.

Pituitary gland A small pea-sized gland at the base of your brain, which tells other glands what to do.

Predator An animal that hunts other animals.

Puberty The process of your body and mind becoming an adult.

Psychological That's a long word! It means anything to do with your brain; like how you are feeling both in your mood and in your body, what you are thinking and what you do.

Rationalizing This is when we try to make sense of things or find a good and clear reason for behaviours or feelings.

Resilience The strength you build to deal with difficult situations.

Secondary emotion An emotion which is often covering up other emotions underneath.

Self-care Anything you do to feel calm, happy or safe.

Self-critical Being really hard on ourselves. We can think that the things we do or say are wrong, think that we haven't done something well enough, or think we aren't good enough.

Self-esteem How you feel about yourself – if you have low self-esteem you might lack confidence and be more negative about yourself. If you have high self-esteem you might like yourself more and be generally more positive about yourself.

Strategy An activity, tool or thought process that you might use to help you handle an emotion or situation.

INDEX